Brainless Sameness

Brainless Sameness

The Demise of One-Size-Fits-All Instruction and the Rise of Competency Based Learning

Bob Sornson

ROWMAN & LITTLEFIELD
Lanham • Boulder • New York • London

Published by Rowman & Littlefield
A wholly owned subsidiary of The Rowman & Littlefield Publishing Group, Inc.
4501 Forbes Boulevard, Suite 200, Lanham, Maryland 20706
www.rowman.com

Unit A, Whitacre Mews, 26–34 Stannary Street, London SE11 4AB

British Library Cataloguing in Publication Information Available

Library of Congress Cataloging-in-Publication Data
ISBN: 978-1-4758-4486-3 (cloth)
ISBN: 978-1-4758-4487-0 (paperback)
ISBN: 978-1-4758-4488-7 (electronic)

♾™ The paper used in this publication meets the minimum requirements of American National Standard for Information Sciences—Permanence of Paper for Printed Library Materials, ANSI/NISO Z39.48–1992.

Printed in the United States of America

Contents

Foreword

Over the past half-century many great educators, recognizing the limitations of our outmoded time-based model of education, have tried diligently to change the system, only to have gone to their graves knowing that the system beat them. But now more than ever there is reason for excitement. A new model is gaining momentum around the country.

It's called competency-based learning, and this model, unlike the many failed reform efforts of the past half-century, is unlikely to get added to the scrap heap of failed reform efforts. The logic is too strong. Instead of measuring time spent in a classroom, this model focuses on student learning. Competency-based learning recognizes that each student is unique, and that students learn at different rates and in different ways. It's going to be better for kids and far more cost-effective than the old model, and there is a growing army of evangelists prepared to build the most effective system of learning ever devised.

During my tenure as chairman of the New Hampshire State Board of Education (2003 to 2012), we were the first in the nation to remove the 180-day requirement from our state regulations and define credit toward graduation, not by hours in a classroom, but by a demonstration of mastery of required competencies. In essence, we replaced time and place as the constants and learning as the variable. Instead students can learn anytime and anyplace, on their path to mastery of a clearly defined learning goal. Mastery/competency/proficiency becomes the constant, while time and place become the variables.

I remember being so excited by what my fellow board members and members of the commissioner's cabinet stumbled upon at the meeting where this epiphany moment happened for us. I came home to tell my educator wife of our discovery. Upon hearing it she said, "I can't believe that no one has thought of this." Well, maybe no one in a position of governing a state's school system, but certainly others outside of American public education have used this model for centuries. Karate instructors, music teachers, and skilled tradesmen figured this out over a thousand years ago.

It shouldn't matter how old you are. You should work on crucial skills and knowledge until mastery, however long it takes. Mastery is defined as the ability to use learned information and skills in known and unknown situations in the future. Once mastery is achieved you then move to the next level.

This is not just a model for high school. Competency-based learning options are flourishing in higher education and in early childhood education. In New Hampshire there is an effort called NG2: No Grades, No Grades. No 1st grade, 2nd grade, 3rd grade. No As, Bs, or Cs. Students work at various skill levels and then move to the next level upon a demonstration of mastery. Currently, this is happening in a number of the state's elementary schools. The effort is being overseen by the New Hampshire Department of Education (NHDOE), and the results have been amazing.

I personally believe that the women and men who have been leading our nation's efforts in public education are honorable, and that most school reform initiatives have been well intentioned. We spend as much money on public education as we do on the U.S. military, and yet it never seems to be enough. The words *boring* and *dropouts* are synonymous with American high schools. Both teachers and students report unhealthy levels of stress. More and more, students and parents around the country are voting with their feet and leaving public education for other options, even if they have to pay for the alternative. This exodus only causes more stress for our already-needy system.

And make no mistake about it. There is damage being done to kids around the country by our continued reliance on an educational system that was designed for mass production. At a time when most industries have learned to offer choice and customization, education has continued to rely on a system that covers the same grade-level curriculum standards for all kids of the same age in a time-limited way. Bob Sornson describes this as Cover-Test-Sort. Cover the material, test the kids, and then assign grades and move on to the next unit of instruction.

The results show up in so many sad stories. Disengaged students. Dropouts. Teacher stress. Angry students. Tragedies around drugs, gangs, and guns. A vast majority of our students nonproficient in reading and math. Does it have to be this way? We all know which students are disengaged, angry, or isolated. Yet too often we simply move these kids through the grades, ignoring their obvious needs because the "system" requires that we cover the next set of grade-level content standards for all kids whether they are ready or not.

So, what are we going to do about it? Are we going to continue to perpetuate a system that has proven for decades that it will not deliver the necessary results? It's time to change the system; not a tweak here or there, but a new model; one that focuses on the personal needs of each student; a customized education for every single child; a move-forward-when-ready model with kids taking ownership of their learning.

My friend Joe DiMartino of the Center for Secondary School Redesign says that "too many in public education pat themselves on the back from the successes of kids who would've been fine without them." That cannot be the legacy of public education. It must become about every student, the hard-to-reach kids and the high-fliers. It must become about helping every kid to have the learning skills needed to be successful in the age of information. It must become about helping students believe in themselves, work well with others, and believe in their ability to build a successful life.

So, what is your role going to be? Are you going to simply read this book and wait for this new thinking to come to a school district near you, or, are you going to do something to speed up the process?

In *Brainless Sameness*, Bob Sornson lays it out with amazing clarity. You will understand why we have our existing traditional system, why it does not and will not work in the modern age, and how with a few strong moves we can redesign our system to meet the needs of individual students. This book, for me, is filled with optimism. We can do this. Vulnerable kids don't need to be left behind. Teachers can become professionals again. Students can realize untapped potential with a system that allows them to move forward based on demonstrated mastery. We can produce a workforce with the real skills to find success in an ever-growing, changing, and learning world. This book offers hope that we can create schools where you would want to be a teacher, and where your kids can become excited about learning.

For those educators, parents, and community leaders who do not yet know about competency-based learning, you have an excuse. You have not yet learned that there is another way, a better way. You may not fully understand the damage that Cover-Test-Sort learning systems inflict. You can be excused for continuing to argue about which list of one-size-fits-all content standards to use, or how to revise the pacing guide, or which teacher-evaluation system to use, or which test to use for your annual standardized state assessment.

But if you read this fine book, you can no longer use ignorance as an excuse. You will understand why the old system can never meet our needs. You will know how to begin the transformation to a new system for learning at every level of school, and throughout life. This could be our legacy: building a nation of learners.

We need you to get involved in bringing this revolution to your schools. The stakes are far too high to sit on the sidelines. There are kids in your district falling through the cracks on a daily basis. We need you to help us create a true competency-based, personalized, customized, student-centered, student-owned education system.

Thank you, Bob Sornson, for lighting the path.

Fred Bramante

Member, New Hampshire Board of Education, 1992 to 1995, 2003 to 2013

Chair, New Hampshire Board of Education, 2003 to 2005

Founder of the National Center for Competency-Based Learning

Coauthor of *Off the Clock: Moving Education from Time to Competency* (with Rose Colby)

Introduction

Four decades of school reform initiatives have drained our optimism. Fool me once, shame on you. Fool me twice, shame on me. Fool me repeatedly with A Nation at Risk, Goals 2000, No Child Left Behind, Standardized Assessment Systems on Steroids, 21st Century Schools, scientifically research-based programming, evidence-based programming, charter school options, privatization, and the Every Student Succeeds Act, and the shame becomes amorphous as we disengage from the belief that any government-led "reform initiative" will produce meaningful results.

Politicians pontificate, fads and educational buzzwords come and go, and islands of educational success fail to move to scale. The pressure on teachers to perform continues to increase, and in turn the pressure on our children increases. Many schools have become joyless places where there is a constant race to "cover" content and test students. Play, beauty, nature, social relationships, self-regulation, character, classroom culture, art, and music suffer the indignity of being marginalized or eliminated from the curriculum.

Poor, minority, brain diverse, and other vulnerable students are exposed to the damage of a system that treats all kids as if they should be ready for one-size-fits-all high-pressure instruction. One-size-fits-all instruction eats neurodiverse and other vulnerable students for lunch.

Without a clear vision for the schools we want for our children there can be no clear plan of action. The shouting begins. Loud voices compete, and thoughtful planning is neglected. The interests of politics, the power of bureaucracies, and the lobbying of the educational industrial complex prevail. School districts cycle through reading and math programs without great success. National Assessment of Educational Progress outcomes are stagnant, and we continue to fall further behind the educational outcomes of other nations.

The general public has become disillusioned and disengaged. It's better not to think about problems over which you have no control. More than 10 million children, about 17 percent of all school-age kids, have left traditional public schools for private schools, charter schools, or homeschooling. In some communities a majority of affluent families have moved away or found alternatives to the public schools. As of 2014, thirty-five states were spending less on education than before the 2008 recession. We've lost confidence in our public schools.

And therefore it is time to choose. Will it be continued disillusionment or fundamental change?

Asking adults to change their thinking and their patterns of behavior can be a fearful thing and much resisted. Opponents of reform contend that poverty is the real problem, rather than what we do in our schools. They argue that using student test results to assess teacher quality is unfair, and that school choice has taken the more motivated students out of traditional public schools. Opponents of fundamental change argue that our schools are already doing the best we can under the circumstances that we are given. They argue (without conviction) that covering a slightly different set of content standards, devising a new and different testing structure, altering the evaluation system we use for teachers, purchasing a new math series, or using a more aggressive pacing guide will somehow lead us to better outcomes.

Fortunately there are a growing number of educators and community leaders who see this as a time of enormous opportunity to build a system designed to meet the needs of individual learners. Rather than blaming the students, the parents, and the teachers for our inadequate results, they see an opportunity to design a system that is built upon a different framework.

"We covered it and tested it" is simply no longer a sufficient premise for a learning system that works in the 21st century. To radically improve learning outcomes for all students, and to ensure that all students have a chance to succeed, we are poised to develop personalized competency-based learning systems that are designed to deliver the outcomes we need in the age of information and learning.

- In creating a model for instruction that better meets the needs of modern learners, we must create a systems architecture that can consistently produce far more **students who love to learn** and continue to learn for life.
- This new systems design must be attentive to the **development of the whole person,** including social-emotional skills, problem-solving skills, and positive character.
- The system must be designed in keeping with everything we know about human learning, and more than lip service must be paid to **instructional match, intrinsic motivation, deep understanding and application, differentiated**

instruction, the importance of safe and connected classroom culture, and the importance of art, music, movement, nature, and beauty.

- This new systems architecture must value **meeting the learning needs of individual students,** rather than giving top priority to covering the content standards du jour.
- The architecture of our new system must abandon "test and sort" in favor of **assessment for learning**. Assessment is most valuable when educators can use that information to thoughtfully design learning for each student, rather than ascribe grades and move on to the next chapter without allowing students to deeply understand and enjoy what they are learning.
- To serve the needs of our children, this systems design must take a radically different view of how to deliver "school," so that **all children**, not just a fortunate few, receive the instruction and practice time to build every essential skill along a pathway to higher-level skills, at their own instructional level, for as long as it takes.

This book offers a careful look at how we came to have our traditional education system, and how it met the needs of a different time. By looking back at the past we can take on the task of change without casting blame, but with understanding. We will consider the systems design of the curriculum-driven, one-size-fits-all educational model, why it no longer meets our needs, and how to devise a system that can deliver a better future for our children and for ourselves as educators.

The most exciting point of this book is that personalized competency-based learning systems are blossoming in every corner of our nation, and in most countries around the world. This is it! The time of greatest innovation, change, learning, collaborating, and constantly improving our schools has begun. There could be no more exciting time to be an educator. The time for rethinking and re-creating our learning systems is now.

Chapter 1

Time for Disruptive Innovation in Our Schools

Decades of "school reform" have produced exactly what? In pursuit of better education outcomes for our children we have continued to rely on a system of teaching that was never designed to help all kids become good learners or love to learn.

During the past several decades of school reform we have debated which content standards to require and how to pressure teachers to cover all the content. We have considered how to assess students at every grade, how to evaluate teachers, and how to rate our schools. But we have never stopped to really consider whether this system has the capacity to help us achieve our goals, and whether it is simply time to upgrade to a different design system that will allow far more of our students to become capable learners for life.

This recalcitrance to change the systems architecture of our schools is especially astounding when we consider the long-standing availability of a different model. Personalized competency-based learning is not a new or unfamiliar concept in our homes, in education for the building trades, driver education, medical education, or in every aspect of technology education. It relies on ongoing observational formative assessment to adjust instruction **so that learners get what they need, at their level, for as long as necessary to achieve complete proficiency**. It offers the promise of much-improved learning outcomes, more joy in the classroom, and the development of students who want to be learners for life.

And yet our schools continue to perseverate on using a one-size-fits-all "coverage" model that dates back to the days of the prairie schooner bumping slowly across the vast expanse of our nation more than 150 years ago.

Brainless Sameness is a call to action:

- To the parents whose children are worthy of a system that taps their potential and inspires a love of learning

1

- To local, state, and national leaders who want to live and work with citizens who have the skills to learn and work, and the character to build strong communities
- To young women and men with the intelligence and skills to teach, who want a system that allows them to be a professional and to be successful opening a world of opportunity to their students
- To education leaders who have grown weary of archaic bureaucratic burdens that limit innovation
- To frustrated learners who want your personal learning needs recognized and addressed by the schools you attend

To create this future, we must first understand our past. The origins of our standardized coverage-based system are linked with good leaders and good intentions. But a system designed for the agrarian and early industrial age cannot adequately serve the children in the age information and learning. Consider this brief history.

The system of education we have been struggling to improve for decades is based on the 1840s Prussian educational system, brought to Massachusetts by Horace Mann, and adapted in the early 1900s to more closely resemble an industrial assembly line. The system is designed to "cover" content, test students, sort them by giving test scores and grades, and then moving on to the next unit or lesson. In the mid-1800s and early 1900s, the use of standardized instruction was a reasonable strategy for a system with limited resources and lack of emphasis on the importance of learning for all students.

Throughout the history of American education, schools relied on local control, based on the belief that parents and community leaders were more responsive to the needs of the children in a community than someone far away in the state capitol. But as the age of technology and innovation emerged during the past half-century, the need for improved student learning outcomes became clearer. States established more regulations, demanded more reports, increased state authority over graduation requirements, and increased testing requirements.

State grade-level content expectations began to guide the development of curriculum, instructional programming, curriculum maps, pacing guides, and district assessment systems. We added more content expectations based on the notion that high-quality teachers "covered" more content with their students. By covering more content we predicted that kids would achieve a better understanding of all the things education experts might put on standardized achievement tests.

But covering more content in our schools did not lead to better learning outcomes on national or international tests. Increased state control, with all the regulations and bureaucracy it created, failed to improve outcomes. We were covering more, and testing more, but our children were not learning more.

The students in some communities were clearly doing better than the students in other communities. Educators in higher-performing communities chose to believe that this was the product of better curriculum and better instruction. In poor communities teachers had similarly covered the content standards, kept up with the pacing guides, completed state and district assessments, and done everything the school reformers had asked without showing positive results. In these communities the students, their parents, and a lack of support for schools were quickly blamed for poor outcomes.

While states were cranking up the pressure in their own way, the disparity between learning outcomes among the states began getting more attention. Each state had its own system of content standards and its own accountability tests. This lack of consistent comparable data made it hard to accurately identify state and local community winners and losers. NCLB (2001) required state testing every year starting in the third grade, and further required that states show annual yearly progress toward improved outcomes. **Many states managed to show "improvement" by simply changing the cut scores on the state tests they managed**. They literally changed the yardstick by which students were named "proficient" so that there was the appearance of greater proficiency without any improvement in learning outcomes. Neat trick!

The manipulation of state data made the system of federal controls and sanctions worthless, and so national school reform leaders quickly moved to develop common standards (CCSS) and common assessment systems. The opportunity to apply for hundreds of millions of Race to the Top and other federal funds was used as an incentive to get states to voluntarily choose to abandon state control over instructional content standards and testing. Forty-five states quickly succumbed and committed to the implementation of national standards and testing systems.

Decades of "school reform" have led us to today. The Common Core State Standard (CCSS) are politically unpopular, and many states have stepped away from them. The national tests, PARCC and Smarter Balance, have produced poor test scores and more students identified as nonproficient. Local districts and states have struggled to accept and defend these scores, and many states have withdrawn their commitment to use these assessment systems. Many experienced educators, having grown tired of the pressure to cover and test, have chosen to leave the profession they love. Many young women and men choose not to become teachers, citing not only the poor pay but also the desire to work within a professional culture that allows them to feel respect and appreciation.

Having listened to political promises to "fix our schools" for so long, the American public is disillusioned. The National Assessment of Educational

Progress (NAEP) and Program for International Student Assessment (PISA) results continue to deliver the bad news that American schools are not improving learning outcomes, and compared to other advanced nations the United States is quickly falling behind.

The Prussian cover-test-sort educational system served it purposes in an agrarian and early industrial society, which was to expose students to a smattering of content and identify a small group as "academically" proficient. But this system is poorly designed to help a large majority of students fall in love with learning, identify what each student needs to learn, allow instruction and support until all basic learning skills are developed, and personalize instruction allowing each student, with effort, to continue to progress at his or her own pace toward higher levels of learning.

Cover content, give tests, and sort students. Our existing system does this effectively, year after year, until a vast majority of our students have been sorted away from the love of learning, sorted away from the economic and social opportunities that are part of the age of innovation, technology, and learning. Poor, minority, and other vulnerable students are especially susceptible to the damage of a system that treats all kids as if they should be ready for one-size-fits-all, high-pressure instruction.

> **So, what is the way forward? The irony is that by choosing to use heavy-handed accountability systems that push us toward an ever more standardized, superficial, fragmented and meaningless learning, we have completely failed to improve test scores and academic learning outcomes. We have stripped away much of the sense of community, joy, play, and social learning from our schools as we hold onto an archaic educational system that was never designed to help large numbers of students become quality learners for life.**

We are overdue for a systems change. For decades as a nation we have clung to this consistently ineffective system. We reformed it by adding content expectations, lots of assessment, and lots of pressure. In recent years we have drained much of the humanity that somehow had managed to survive by the grace of good teachers and curious learners. All that is left is a race to cover dry, personally meaningless facts and concepts that might be included on a standardized test so that some bureaucrat can pretend that our results are better than dismal.

Given the demands of the standardized learning systems architecture, it is amazing that some schools (not all) have managed to hold onto a humane culture, find a few moments in which teachers can build caring relationships with their students, and work so hard to inspire their students to love learning. Imagine what these educators could do within a system that is purposefully designed to create a nation of learners!

It is time for a systems change to a personalized system of learning that allows far more students to become good learners and great people. Such a system is based on far different design specifications that are based on considerably more accurate assumptions about human learning:

- At the same age, all students are not alike in their experiences, rates of development, and learning readiness.
- Some students need more time to learn a concept or skill, but are fully capable of learning well if given sufficient time.
- All students learn better when offered instruction at a level of challenge that allows for high rates of success.
- Students work better in a community in which they feel safe and connected to others.
- Paying attention to the development of the whole child recognizes the importance of social-emotional intelligence and also supports academic learning.
- Pushing kids into a frustration zone, in the name of academic rigor, causes them to disengage from learning, stop trying, and even misbehave and disrupt the classroom.

In the 1840s the prairie schooner was the vehicle of choice for travel on the Oregon Trail, an overland route between Missouri and the Pacific Northwest and California. The box of the schooner was about four feet wide and eleven feet long. Its cover was made of cotton canvas, and it had no suspension. The schooner was pulled by teams of horses, mules, or oxen, and its average rate of travel was about two miles per hour. At about this same time we began to use the Prussian model of standardized grade-level curriculum with students in American schools, exposing them to a little bit of reading, math, and civics. Only a very few students stayed in school for more than a few years, most of them seeing that academic learning was not particularly important for their lives.

Today we live in a world in which learning matters for all our students. While our vehicles for transportation have changed enormously, and we see the results of transformational innovation in almost all aspects of our lives, schools have remained resistant to significant change in the way we deliver instruction. We still focus on making lists of content standards for all kids in the same grade. We offer one-size-fits-all instruction, and use grades to identify better students. We manage to help a few students become self-motivated and successful learners, but allow a vast majority to experience learning frustration and disengagement.

In the 1840s Horace Mann established a system of public education that reasonably served the community learning needs of those times. But for the past fifty years our education system has been failing a vast majority of our students, failing to keep up with the advancement in other nations, and failing to help students develop skills for success in the age of information and technology.

We are overdue for a systems change, and we need the shining stars, the innovators, the change-makers, and the world-shakers to overcome entrenched barriers to innovation and build a new model of purposeful and joyful learning for life.

We need educators who refuse to be dumbed down, deprofessionalized, and demeaned by standardized one-size-fits-all one-best-way scripted and rigidly paced instructional systems.

We need leaders who are ready to innovate, who will not accept a system that is failing our vulnerable students.

We need builders who will make the long-term commitment to construct systems that are more humane, more equitable, and far more effective for all learners.

We need thoughtful men and women who won't accept flimsy excuses or pathetic political responses to questions that challenge the status quo.

Will we hold onto the idea that all students should be ready to learn the standard content on the same day and in the same way, or are we ready to acknowledge that we are all different in our development and that serving the learning needs of children requires us to develop our ability to personalize learning to allow for the amazing diversity among our students?

Will we continue to work in schools modeled after factories from a bygone era, or do we commit to rediscovering the joy of great teaching and learning and building systems that connect discovery, learning, and joy?

Will we continue the falsehood that somehow with yet another list of one-size-fits-all content standards or the newest assessment system we will eventually bring improved outcomes? Or will we step beyond those fallacies and design a system that respects individual difference and values the development of the whole child?

We have an abundance of science to help us understand the different ways in which children develop and learn. We have the technologies to track individual development and support crucial learning at each child's instructional level. We have the capacity to build learning systems in which:

- practically all students become successful readers and mathematicians
- individual students find and develop their unique core of interests and aptitudes
- learners develop the social-emotional intelligence to understand themselves and others
- children develop the grit and character needed to build lives of purpose

How long will we wait?

Chapter 2

Our Moment of Opportunity

Disruptive innovations are new ways of doing things that disrupt or overturn the traditional methods and practices. Steam engines in the age of sailing vessels. Internet in the age of postal mail. Digital photography in the age of film. The term was first defined and analyzed by Clayton Christensen and his collaborators (1997, 2004, 2006), and is one of the most influential ideas of the 21st century.

Technology offers new options to us that allow far more personalization of the learning process, but that is only one part of the impetus toward competency-based learning. Christensen defined disruptive innovation as a product or service designed for a new set of customers. The learning needs of a child in the 21st century are different from those of children whose families were traveling west in a prairie schooner. The real power of competency-based learning is that it opens up the potential for so many more people to become successful learners for life.

No longer do we live in an age in which a small set of readers, mathematicians, and problem-solvers are sufficient for the social and economic needs of our society. To live productive lives, our children need to be skilled at learning, collaborating with others, and managing themselves in a complex society. Old thinking about standardized one-size-fits-all schooling no longer serves our children.

The need is clear, and the opportunity for change is everywhere around us. As you will see in future chapters, there are models of competency-based learning that have been with us for centuries, other models that are emerging at every level of learning, and other models that are built into the digital devices and games that surround us.

In building learning systems for the future, we are not restricted by the thinking built into the Cover Test Sort (CTS) school design of the past. **Instead imagine the learning systems of the future:**

1. In every domain of human learning there will be clear pathways to higher levels of learning. Beginning with clear concise learning goals that are foundational to ongoing progress, students will progress at their own personal rate toward higher-level skills. No crucial steps will be skipped. While some students will progress more quickly, every student will know that continued learning success in any learning domain is available with more time and effort.

   Contrast this with our existing system that standardizes curriculum by grade and course. Students with varied learning needs and developmental readiness are exposed to the same material at the same pace of instruction. Tests follow each unit, followed by grades that compare learning outcomes, labeling some students as high-achievers and others as low-achievers. These ratings impact each student's belief that he or she is "good" or "bad" at this subject matter, and are now understood to be a poor motivator for greater effort. In most cases, students who struggle in a subject over time begin to disengage from effort and learning in that domain.

2. On any given day, students and teachers will know precisely where each student is on the skill development continuum. In the early years, it will be clear which phonologic skills, oral language skills, motor skills, self-regulation and behavior skills, literacy, and numeracy are fully developed and competent, and which skills need more time practice and instruction. As students grow older, teachers and students will share an understanding of each student's math development, writing skills, speaking skill levels, collaboration skills, science skill development, and a precise understanding of each student's reading skills.

   Contrast this with the far more vague understanding that comes with knowing that a student is a "B"-level reader or mathematician. Delivery of standardized curriculum is followed by the assignment of grades. Knowing students' precise learning skills and needs makes it possible for teachers and students to identify and focus on the next necessary step toward high-level skills.

3. Knowing each student's skill level allows instruction to be designed daily, which matches student learning readiness. Instruction that is too easy becomes boring to the learner. Instruction that is too difficult causes learners to shut down. Both of these patterns over time produce poor

habits of learning. Finding the sweet spot at which students are challenged but not overwhelmed is commonly understood as the instructional zone, instructional match, or zone of proximal development. This is the instructional experience that maximizes student engagement, motivation, and learning.

Contrast this with the delivery of standardized grade-level content objectives. All students in a given grade are given the same content using the same rigid pacing guide. Reliance on this model ensures "coverage," which for many years has been the first priority of our standardized grade-level learning design. This is the model that systematically devours vulnerable children and causes fortunate learners to become bored and lazy.

4. In the competency-based learning systems of the future, teachers will know the learning levels of their students, design instruction that matches their needs, and then carefully monitor progress to see if each student has managed to progress to a higher level. The priority for assessment will be to better understand the learning needs of each student rather than to label them as "A-" or "C-" level learners. When teaching children to catch a ball you might throw to the right, or throw to the left, or toss a slight pop-up. Then you observe carefully to see how they catch the ball. You don't give them a "D" grade every time they drop the ball. Instead, you monitor progress and adjust your throws so there is just the right level of challenge. A good teacher makes learning to catch challenging, exciting, and highly successful.

Contrast this to the delivery of a standardized unit of instruction, followed by a test and a grade. In the traditional standardized learning system, teachers are told to prioritize squeezing all the content expectations into the plan for coverage. In the competency-based learning system teachers prioritize monitoring individual progress and adjusting their instruction to match the learning needs of each child. This is the new "rigor" we will see in our schools.

5. In future learning systems, students will advance upon demonstrated mastery. This mastery will represent deep understanding of a skill or knowledge, along with the capacity to use it successfully in multiple contexts. This is a much higher standard for mastery/proficiency/competency than has been used in the past. Getting 80 percent on a multiple-choice test does not show mastery. Mastery is the real deal, acknowledging that any important skill has been learned deeply, is available for use in multiple contexts, and is unlikely to be forgotten.

Contrast this with learning systems today that cover so much content with so little depth, and push kids forward with pathetically poor levels of understanding. Imagine really understanding all basic number skills that allow you to understand higher levels of math. Imagine learning science not by memorizing formulas and definitions for a test, but by understanding the beauty and complexity of real science.

6. The learning systems of the future will consider any pattern of allowing students to sit through lesson they have already learned as a colossal waste of time. The learning systems of the future will consider allowing students to be overwhelmed, frustrated, and pushed into disengagement from the learning process to be cruel, unethical, and behavior akin to criminal. Whether digital, blended, or classroom-based, essential learning skills and content will be individualized. Whole-group instruction will still be a part of the learning process, with small segments of content available from great teachers, and with collaborative- and project-based learning serving as a way to make abstract content come to life.

   Contrast this with the many one-size-fits-all learning systems, with rigid pacing guides, and with scripted learning programs that can be found in typical schools.

7. In the age of information and innovation being a strong learner is a precondition for success now and in the foreseeable future. Competency-based learning systems make learning always available to students. Students are never pushed forward without mastery of essential skills needed for success at higher levels. Students are never labeled as low-quality learners. Vulnerable students who struggle to keep up are given the extra time and instruction they need. More fortunate students who were enriched at home or gifted with early learning success will not be given honors for getting good grades without giving any effort. Learning will be a process, always available, responsive to time and effort, for life. This is the essence of a growth mind-set, the belief that you can identify learning goals to improve your life or your world and then make progress toward those goals with effort and persistence.

   Contrast this with a design for learning in which by the third grade, most students have decided that some subjects are easy and others are hard because success does not come easily. A few weeks, perhaps a few months, certainly a few years of frustration in a subject area is enough for most students to lose the growth mind-set. Once lost, it is difficult to recover.

8. Competency-based learning systems prioritize meaningful assessment that informs both the teacher and the student. Teachers are informed by

formative assessment to better understand their students. Is it time to move forward to higher levels of challenge? Does my student need additional practice, more instruction, a different style of instruction? Students are informed by understanding what they can do in comparison with clear standards for learning. They have clear learning goals, whether learning to catch a ball, or learning to fully understand mathematical combinations up to 30. It becomes easy to compare your skills today with the standards for competency that will allow you to advance to higher-level skills. With clear learning goals, and with an absolute knowledge that they will have the support needed to achieve these goals, students accept ownership and maintain self-efficacy as a learner.

Contrast this with students who do as little as possible to get a passing grade, or with students who passively accept vague learning goals that are associated with covering content about which the students are entirely indifferent. Years of practicing "school" leaves many students unable to identify anything they sincerely want to learn.

9. In the schools of the future, students will have a say in what they learn and how they learn it. Clearly defined learning goals that lead to higher-level skills do not need to be learned in the same way, or at the same pace, as all other students. Successful competency-based learning systems will identify what a student knows, and what they are ready to learn. And they will also recognize that students have wonderfully divergent styles of learning, different motivators, and different interests. The art of devising classrooms and schools in the future will include carefully monitoring student progress, but also know how to excite and engage an individual's connection to learning.

   Contrast this with a curriculum based on covering grade-level content expectations in a one-size-fits-all drill and kill rigidly paced and graded instructional system. Yes, that is the one we are typically using.

10. In the schools of the future, teachers will have clear content expectations and pathways leading to higher-level skills, know their students, give them instruction at their level of readiness, carefully monitor progress and adapt instruction, and advance students based on mastery. And to make this really work they will acknowledge student differences and help students take ownership of their own learning. Academic rigor will be defined as knowing your students and engaging them in meaningful work at their instructional level. And all this will take place within a safe community of learners where the love of learning is cultivated.

   Contrast this with the typical school experience of American students and so many students around the world.

And in this extraordinary moment of opportunity it is possible to create far more respectful and effective learning systems at every level and in every community. As you will see in these chapters, it is already beginning to happen in every corner of the nation and across the world.

We have not yet begun to consider our full capacity for human learning. This potential is limited only by the degree to which thoughtful leaders embrace change, and then design and build systems that support far healthier outcomes for our children.

Chapter 3

Hasn't Worked Can't Work Won't Work

Cover content, give tests, and sort students. Our existing system of instruction does this effectively, in much the same way now as it did in the early 1900s, and in much the same way as it did in the 1840s, when Horace Mann brought the Prussian model of education to Massachusetts and to our nation.

Cover. The system we use spends a lot of time considering what should be "covered." We've developed a rich vocabulary of terms, including syllabus, scope and sequence, lesson plans, content expectations, grade-level content standards, Common Core State Standards, Texas Teaching Standards, course description, curriculum map, and curriculum. They all refer to what will be "covered" in a course or in a grade.

In most modern schools, Coverage is King. Teachers strive to "cover" all the content expectations that may be included in a state assessment or in their own district assessment. Teachers have succumbed to the steady demand to "cover," even when they know many of their students are confused, struggling, or disengaged. **It must be covered** is the almost unquestioned expectation. Pacing guides define the rate of delivery.

The students will range in age and developmental readiness, language, self-regulation, and social-emotional skills. Some will come from poverty, while others will be from affluence and privilege. Student ages will vary by at least one year, and the group will include both boys and girls. We will take this incredibly diverse group of children, put a large number of them in a classroom with one teacher, require the teacher to deliver standardized one-size-fits-all instruction while ignoring the different learning needs and readiness of his or her students.

Test. We cover the material using a time-limited instructional system. Students who might be capable of deeply understanding content and skills with additional instruction and practice will not get that additional time. Instead, it is time for testing. After each unit there is a test, which gives each student a grade, and then all students move forward in the curriculum at the pace dictated by the pacing guide.

In some disciplines, like mathematics, it is especially obvious how badly one-size-fits-all instruction and testing is failing our kids. Lacking deep understanding of essential math skills, students are encouraged to memorize facts and formulas they do not understand. Without basic number sense, many students learn to hate and avoid math. More than a third of our students end up in remedial math courses, and high levels of math anxiety are reported among school-aged children, beginning in the earliest grades. Many students report that math is their least favorite subject.

In recent decades, our time-limited one-size-fits-all system of instruction and testing has added the additional pressure of mandated standardized testing, first by state mandate and eventually by national mandates. We deliver more content than is reasonable in the time available, hoping that by "covering" the standards that might be included on the mandated assessments our students will get better test scores. We compare students by giving grades, and so we begin to compare schools, districts, and states by test scores as well.

Teachers teach to the test. Precious instructional time is given to test preparation and to the process of state and district assessment. **The irony is that by choosing to use heavy-handed accountability systems that push us toward an ever more standardized, superficial, fragmented, and meaningless learning, we have completely failed to improve test scores and academic learning outcomes**. We have stripped away much of the sense of community, joy, play, and social learning from our schools as we hold onto an archaic educational system that was never designed to help large numbers of students become quality learners for life.

Sort. We sort students by percentile rankings on state achievement tests and standardized reading and math tests. We sort them by grades on report cards and on end-of-unit tests. But mostly we sort them by the success they find or fail to find day in and day out in our classrooms.

Students who are fortunate to be fully ready for grade-level instruction may spend time learning easily or with a small modicum of effort. But many students are not fully ready for grade-level instruction, whether by age, stress, lack of self-regulation, developmental delays, mild auditory or visual processing disorders, poor home experiences, or difficulty sustaining attention for classroom learning. Some children, no matter how hard they might try, cannot keep up with the pace of classroom instruction. When instruction falls into their frustration zone, these students quickly disengage from learning and identify themselves as poor in a subject area, or poor at learning in general.

Cover content, give tests, and sort students. Our existing system does this effectively, year after year, until a vast majority of our students have been sorted away from the love of learning, sorted away from the economic and social opportunities that are part of the age of innovation, technology, and learning. Poor and minority students are especially vulnerable to the damage of a system that treats all kids as if they should be ready for one-size-fits-all, high-pressure instruction.

As an observer and participant in this education system, the most amazing thing to me is how tenaciously we hold onto a model that offers such limited success. Many students find it tedious and boring, while many others experience difficulty and frustration. The CTS education model was never designed to help all students become successful learners. It may have generally served the needs of society in the late 19th and early 20th centuries, but in recent decades, as it has become more important for us to develop the academic and problem-solving skills that lead to good jobs and social opportunity, the CTS education model is failing our society.

Figure 3.1.   Pixabay photo by Greyerbaby , CC0 1.0, Pixabay 529067

All students are limited by standardized one-size-fits-all instruction, but it is a special catastrophe for vulnerable children who are less able to keep up with the pace of instruction.

- By the beginning of fourth grade only **34 percent of American children are at proficient reading levels** (National Assessment of Educational Progress, 2013)

- Only **20 percent** of fourth-grade children who are eligible for **free or reduced lunch** are at proficient reading levels (National Assessment of Educational Progress, 2013)
- Among twelfth-grade students—remember that a significant group of students has already dropped out by this point—26 percent score at or above proficient levels in math, and 38 percent are proficient or better in reading (National Assessment of Educational Progress, 2013)
- Among **African American twelfth-grade students tested, 7 percent** are proficient or better in math and 16 percent are proficient or better in reading (National Assessment of Educational Progress, 2013)
- Each year about a million students leave high school without a diploma

Since the early 1970s, the NAEP has monitored student-learning outcomes in each state and across the nation. After all the political shouting, after all the school reform initiatives, after all the billions of dollars spent on school reform, NAEP longitudinal data shows no significant progress for seventeen-year-old American students. Results on international tests are similarly dismal, showing no progress at all for U.S. students over the years PISA has been administered.

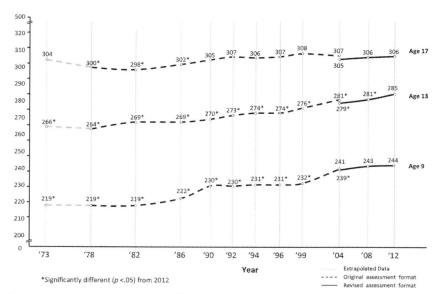

*Significantly different (p <.05) from 2012

Figure 3.2. NAEP Long-Term Reading Trends, Average Scaled Scores *Source:* **National Assessment of Educational Progress, The Nation's Report Card: Trends in Academic Progress, 2012.**

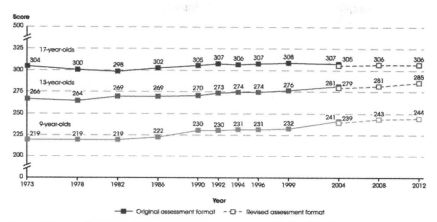

Figure 3.3. NAEP Long-Term Math Trends, Average Scaled Scores *Source*: National Assessment of Educational Progress, The Nation's Report Card: Trends in Academic Progress, 2012.

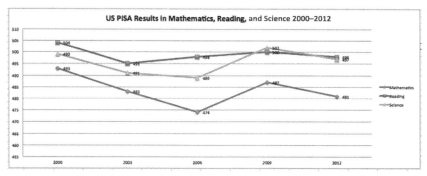

Figure 3.4. PISA Long-Term Math, Reading, and Science, Average Scaled Scores for U.S. students *Source*: Program for International Student Assessment, 2013.

Between 2010 and 2015 the U.S. Department of Education awarded more than $7 billion in school improvement grants (SIG) to "turn around" struggling schools. As the latest in a long series of federal and state turnaround school reform initiatives, SIG was offered as a solution to reform for around 5,000 failing schools. Individual schools could receive up to $2 million per year for three years, based on the adoption of one of the administration's four preferred reforms: replacing the principal and at least half the teachers, converting into a charter school, closing altogether, or undergoing a "transformation," including hiring a new principal and adopting new instructional strategies, new teacher evaluations, and a longer school day.

But the final IES report (2017) on the SIG initiative delivered more bad news. None of the reform strategies showed a significant positive effect. SIG didn't improve math scores. Or reading scores. Or high school graduation rates. Or college enrollment.

And still we continue to perseverate on which list of content standards we should require teachers to "cover," which standardized system assessment should be used to sort student outcomes, and how to grade schools and teachers as they work in systems designed to cover, test, and sort. We blindly hold onto a one-size-fits-all system that hasn't worked, can't work, and won't work to serve the learning needs of our children.

"We covered it and tested it" is simply no longer a sufficient premise for a learning system that works in the 21st century. It is time for a systems change.

Chapter 4

Designing Student Learning for the 21st Century

The learning system we've used in our country since the 1840s does exactly what it is designed to do. Brought to us from Prussia in the days when settlers traveled across America in prairie schooners, this system establishes standard grade-level curricula to be delivered by teachers, and asks them to cover the content, test the students, and then move forward to the next lesson or unit. The system worked well enough to expose students to some basic reading, math, civics, and American culture in the days when higher levels of academic skill were not needed for most jobs and only a small fraction of students were expected to stay in school and graduate from high school. Much like the prairie schooner, it served its purpose in those times.

Figure 4.1. Public Domain, NARA-286056 Carriage

21

By the 1890s the days of the prairie schooner were numbered. Mechanized forms of travel began to replace the wagon and team that had so dutifully carried settlers across the plains and mountains. But the education system has continued to hold onto the same standardized delivery of instruction during the industrial age, the advent of the automobile, during the Depression of the 1930s, during world wars, the nuclear age, and the age of information and technology, during more than a century of incredible change.

After World War II greater attention was given to the importance of learning. Scientific advances had made it clear that nations with more advanced learners would have an advantage in business, manufacturing, science, and military defense. But our standardized model of schooling persisted, even while schools began to feel extra pressure to achieve better learning outcomes.

Oxen, horses, mules, and wagons have given way to gasoline, diesel, and electric engines. Railroads, automobiles, motorcycles, airplanes, and jets have transformed our transportation systems, while schools have doubled down on standardized one-size-fits-all delivery of instruction.

Computers systems connect us to more information than we could ever process. A typical smartphone holds more computer power than all of NASA at the time of the moon launch in 1969. Our smartphones know where we are and what we buy, and offer us directions or suggestions for lunch. And while all this transformation continues, our schools debate which list of standards to "cover" for all students in the same grade, and which set of tests to use to compare student outcomes, school outcomes, state outcomes, and national outcomes.

We now live in the greatest era of information and innovation in the history of humanity. And we continue to hold onto a model of instruction that is designed to cover, test, sort students into winners and losers and then move forward in the standardized curriculum. Even while models of competency-based learning are all around us, we have held onto our educational prairie schooner rather than innovating and changing into a model that is far more effective for the vast majority of students.

We continue to cover and test, and then we sort students and schools into winners and losers. Our outcomes are consistently dismal, decade after decade, using a system that covers, tests, and moves on. We leave children behind, with incomplete understanding of crucial content and skills, with every grade and every class.

Let's offer a rationale for why we have so unrelentingly held on to a cover-test-sort educational model. Until recent decades access to information and learning resources was limited. Not so long ago, we really believed the world's collected knowledge could be captured in a twenty-six-volume encyclopedia. Textbooks were the best source of information for teaching and learning. Cost and availability limited us to using standardized textbooks and learning systems. Curriculum-driven instruction gave every child the same

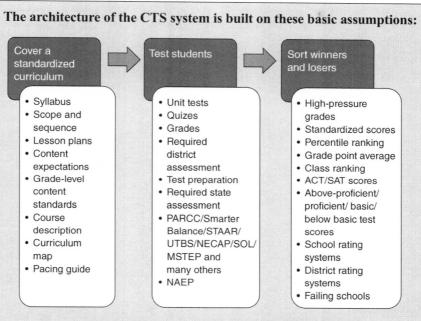

The architecture of the CTS system is built on these basic assumptions:

Cover a standardized curriculum

- Syllabus
- Scope and sequence
- Lesson plans
- Content expectations
- Grade-level content standards
- Course description
- Curriculum map
- Pacing guide

Test students

- Unit tests
- Quizes
- Grades
- Required district assessment
- Test preparation
- Required state assessment
- PARCC/Smarter Balance/STAAR/ UTBS/NECAP/SOL/ MSTEP and many others
- NAEP

Sort winners and losers

- High-pressure grades
- Standardized scores
- Percentile ranking
- Grade point average
- Class ranking
- ACT/SAT scores
- Above-proficient/ proficient/ basic/ below basic test scores
- School rating systems
- District rating systems
- Failing schools

In the Cover/Test/Sort Instructional Model

All students will receive basically the same content and instruction during a grade level or course, regardless of developmental variance and history of educational success, regardless of whether they have the foundation skills needed for deep understanding and application of the knowledge or skills to be covered.

Students will receive time-limited instruction for coverage of a unit, lesson, or course. Available learning time is limited to the duration of the course or unit. Students will then be tested and graded to demonstrate who was more successful. Achievement varies by student and is reflected by a grade.

A high-pressure environment is used to get teachers to cover more content and to get students to achieve better on standardized tests of the standardized curricula.

Figure 4.2. Cover Test Sort Systems Assumptions

opportunity to grasp the content. Textbooks and lesson plans and tests at the end of each unit were simply how schools worked.

Textbooks and encyclopedias are no longer the best available sources of information. Access to information is ubiquitous. The world's knowledge is increasing at an exponential rate. Information technologies allow us to track personal learning information, offer choice, and recognize individual differences. But lacking a clear vision for a different system for learning, we hold onto the system we know.

> **That's how schools work.**
> **It was good enough for me.**
> **It's a law, a regulation,**
> **it's required.**

We have consistently failed to personalize our education systems. After decades and billions of dollars of "school reform" we have managed to keep right on using the same basic design for our educational systems. We engage in rancorous discussions about what to "cover," but one-size-fits-all time-limited coverage is still our basic design for instruction. We allow political lobbying and manipulation to dictate how we will "test" our children, and then we ascribe test scores, compare children by percentile scores, and sort out the winners from the losers. We continue to produce a relatively small group of "winners" who have solid understanding of foundation skills and love to learn.

Science, technology, information, and innovation have changed our world dramatically in every aspect of life, except in our schools.

Treating all kids the same is not treating all kids fairly, equally, or optimizing learning for anyone. One-size-fits-all has never been the dominant instructional approach in career and technical education, digital learning, medical school, sports training, or learning in the home. Everybody knows how to personalize learning when it comes to teaching their kids to walk, swim, cook, catch a ball, or ride a bike.

You may choose to blame the unions for this lack of innovation, the local school boards for their complacency and unwillingness to demand more, dim-witted politicians for their puffery and willingness to spend our money without accountability, teachers for their lack of leadership and professionalism, or parents who are raising their kids amid a confusing culture and whose children are poorly self-regulated and failing to fall in love with learning.

But really the blame belongs to all of us who know that learning skills are crucial to the lives of our children and yet tolerate an educational system that is clearly not serving the needs of so many children, especially vulnerable children whose lack of learning skills and work skills will diminish their lives in so many ways. **We tolerate a system of education in which:**

- Teachers are trained to write lesson plans for the whole class, cover the curriculum, and deliver instruction to all kids in the same time frame.
- Content coverage is prioritized over competency.
- People in leadership have vested interests in holding onto a system they know rather than pursuing a system about which they may not be considered an expert.
- Textbook, activity book, and materials providers are anxious to hold the market share they have worked so hard to achieve.
- Standardized tests provide an incomplete and unreliable assessment of student performance and are used as a club to sort students, schools, districts, and states without giving valuable data to suggest how to improve outcomes.
- Complex government bureaucracies grow, spawning regulations and requirements that suck the vitality out of school district administrators and teachers who are trying to learn, collaborate, and innovate.
- Government and school district bureaucrats hold tightly to control the system they know rather than re-invent or relinquish their role of oversight in a personalized competency-based learning system.

We've avoided meaningful innovation and improvement for more than a century, and we have a lot of catching up to do. For those thoughtful educators, community leaders, parents, and grandparents who still believe this task is possible, it is time to step up and speak up. Every year another crop of beautiful children, with the potential to live successful and meaningful lives, fall into the frustration and disengagement from learning that will profoundly diminish their future.

"We covered it and tested it" in a one-size-fits-all time-limited educational system is a poor excuse for a learning systems architecture in the 21st century. **Fortunately we are surrounded by examples of personalized**

competency-based learning systems, some of which have been around for a very long time.

The Girl Scouts and Boy Scouts devised a merit badge system that is competency-based and dates back to the early 1900s. Preparation for the trades, including electricians, plumbers, carpenters, and steelworkers, has long used a mastery-based apprentice to journeyman to master-level progression of skills based on competency. Music, fine arts, medical, and martial arts training programs help their students build skills one step at a time, guiding them along a pathway to higher-level skills.

In the digital age technical training in IT and many related disciplines is personalized and competency-based. Digital game designers use a deep understanding of human learning and motivation to devise games and programs that engage the participant and keep him or her in the zone. Many universities are moving quickly toward competency-based learning, following the lead of Western Governors University, Capella, and others.

New Hampshire and Maine have led the way toward competency-based high school graduation systems, which replace antiquated course and Carnegie credit requirements. Early childhood programs in Michigan, Mississippi, and around the world are using the *Essential Skill Inventories* (Sornson, 2012) as a PK to Grade 3 competency framework. These concise inventories identify the foundation skills that students must deeply understand and be able to use to allow continued progress toward higher levels of learning.

There are so many ways in which a redesigned system has the potential to quickly improve learning outcomes for our children:

1. In creating a model for instruction that better meets the needs of modern learners, we will create a systems architecture that can consistently produce far more **students who love to learn** and continue to learn for life.
2. This new systems design will be attentive to the **development of the whole person,** including social-emotional skills, problem-solving skills, and positive character.
3. The system will be designed in keeping with everything we know about human learning, and more than lip service must be paid to **instructional match, intrinsic motivation, deep understanding and application, differentiated instruction, the importance of safe and connected classroom culture, and the importance of art, music, movement, nature, and beauty**.
4. This new systems architecture will value **meeting the learning needs of individual students**, rather than giving top priority to covering the content standards du jour.
5. The architecture of our new system will abandon "test and sort" in favor of **assessment for learning**. Assessment is most valuable when educators

can use that information to thoughtfully design learning for each student, rather than ascribe grades and move on to the next chapter without allowing students to deeply understand and enjoy what they are learning.

6. To serve the needs of our children, this systems design will take a radically different view of how to deliver "school," so that **all children**, not just a fortunate few, receive the instruction and practice time to build every essential skill along a pathway to higher-level skills, at their own instructional level, for as long as it takes. **In the age of information, technology, and the rapid exchange of ideas, learning matters for all our students.** Without good learning skills, students are relegated to low-skill, low-wage lives with limited economic and social options. Without better learning systems, vulnerable children will continue to fall behind; disengage from learning; fail to develop the literacy, numeracy, and social-emotional skills needed for economic and social success. Without better learning systems we will see wider gaps between rich and poor, opportunity and indignity, confidence in a better world for our children or the resignation to disillusion and despair.

Our challenge is to create personalized competency-based learning systems which:

- allow practically all students to become successful readers and mathematicians
- help individual students find and develop their unique core of interests and aptitudes
- value the development of social-emotional intelligence and character
- help young men and women build lives of purpose

The prairie schooner was lovely in its own way, but today there are better ways to travel. The educational systems design we continue to use in our schools is every bit as archaic as the schooner, traveling two miles an hour across the prairies. It is time for a systems update. Are you ready to dig in and make it happen?

The architecture of a Competency-Based Learning system is built on significantly different assumptions:

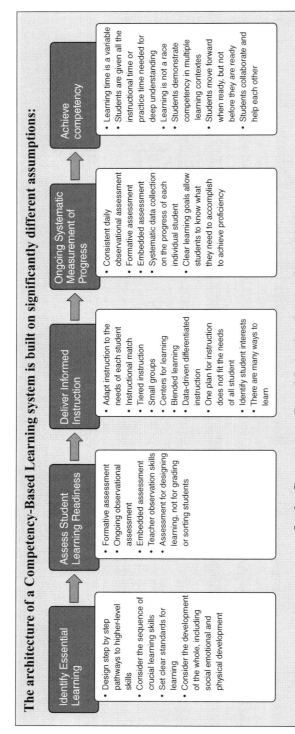

Identify Essential Learning	Assess Student Learning Readiness	Deliver Informed Instruction	Ongoing Systematic Measurement of Progress	Achieve competency
• Design step by step pathways to higher-level skills • Consider the sequence of crucial learning skills • Set clear standards for learning • Consider the development of the whole, including social emotional and physical development	• Formative assessment • Ongoing observational assessment • Embedded assessment • Teacher observation skills • Assessment for designing learning, not for grading or sorting students	• Adapt instruction to the needs of each student • Instructional match • Tiered instruction • Small groups • Centers for learning • Blended learning • Data-driven differentiated instruction • One plan for instruction does not fit the needs of all student • Identify student interests • There are many ways to learn	• Consistent daily observational assessment • Formative assessment • Embedded assessment • Systematic data collection on the progress of each individual student • Clear learning goals allow students to know what they need to accomplish to achieve proficiency	• Learning time is a variable • Students are given all the instructional time or practice time needed for deep understanding • Learning is not a race • Students demonstrate competency in multiple learning contexts • Students move forward when ready, but not before they are ready • Students collaborate and help each other

In the Competency-Based Learning Instructional Model

Students advance upon mastery, not time.

At the same age, all students are not alike in their experiences, rates of development, and learning readiness.

Students receive instruction and support based on need, not based on age or a pacing guide.

All students learn better when offered instruction at a level of challenge that allows for high rates of success.

Students work better in a community in which they feel safe and connected to others.

Figure 4.3. Competency-Based Learning Systems Assumptions

Chapter 5

Personalized Competency-Based Learning in Elementary and Preschool

They come in many shapes, sizes, and colors. Some have experienced rich and interesting learning experiences at home, with high-quality family routines, secure attachments, and a strong sense of safety and connection, while others live with insecurity, anger, and chaos. Some have enjoyed thousands of hours of interactive play, rich language experiences, excellent nutrition, time with nature, art, and music, while others have had limited exposure to good language and social models. These patterns account for some of the differences in readiness for school when children begin preschool or kindergarten.

Additional differences in school readiness are based on the twelve-month age difference among incoming students. Gender is associated with different levels of language skills, visual-motor skills, and social readiness. Diverse learning needs may be associated with second-language learners, kids who have never owned a box of crayons, never used scissors for projects, or never played a musical instrument. Some neurodiversity rises to the level of diagnosis, but so much of the diversity among children when they come to school is unlabeled.

> **Kids are different. They develop at different rates and in different ways. Vygotsky, Piaget, Erikson, Gesell, Bowlby, Montessori, Gardner, Maslow, and other theorists help us understand and appreciate these differences. Everyone who has ever worked with young children can attest to the developmental variance and different learning needs of young children.**

And then these diverse children come to the typical school, that place in which all students are expected to be ready for grade-level content standards to be covered and tested in a time-limited learning system. One-size-fits-all instruction and assessment quickly sorts kids into winners and losers. By the end of the third grade, the last of the early childhood years, children have settled into patterns of learning that usually persist for life.

Imagine this scenario. Bradley is entering kindergarten. He was a low-birth-weight premature baby, born to a young single mother who had few resources. Her pregnancy was filled with stress from her personal life and her heavy work schedule, trying to manage two jobs. After birth, Bradley was quickly placed into the least-expensive childcare available so his mom could try to support herself and her baby. Less than optimal childcare, poor nutrition, high levels of maternal stress, and a lack of predictable routines at home have impacted Bradley. He is an anxious boy, sometimes angry and defiant, with a limited attention span, who does not play well with others. He avoids visual motor activities, and is slightly awkward in his movement patterns, with limited vocabulary, not much empathy, and poor social skills. And he is going to kindergarten because he just turned five, on the last day of August, and he will be the youngest child in his class.

Kindergarten, some have said, is the new first grade. That means that instead of the old-style kindergarten, a place for getting comfortable with school behaviors and routines, a place filled with play centers and building blocks, a place with lots of time for stories, music, and nature, Bradley's kindergarten has "high expectations."

In Bradley's kindergarten children are expected to come in ready to learn. They will "cover" every one of the Common Core Standards. The teacher has a pacing guide and is expected to keep up with the rigorous schedule required to cover every lesson and standard. District assessment will take place quarterly, to ensure that the teacher has kept up with the expected pace of instruction. Most of the lessons in this classroom are one-size-fits-all whole-group instruction.

Everyone does the same math lesson every day. There are few manipulatives. The teacher reads from a scripted narrative, models the math activity of the day, and then gives the daily assignment to all kids in the class. Some children understand the math concepts easily and finish the assignment within a few minutes. Others struggle to understand the lesson but persist. Others are quickly frustrated, lose focus, disengage, and sometimes begin to misbehave. Bradley is usually a part of this latter group.

Most readers are very familiar with this pattern, and how it plays out. Each grade level has a standard curriculum, built to cover standardized content expectations. Teachers are monitored to ensure that it all gets "covered" in a misguided effort to improve test scores on the state-standardized annual assessment. Bradley's teacher may make Herculean efforts to connect with her students and help them build the essential skills they need, but the system limits her ability to have time for many of the needs she observes, and limits her ability to offer instruction that is not in line with the pacing guide.

This standardized instructional system is not likely to work for Bradley because he is unable to learn much of the content that is presented. His language skills, motor skills, self-regulation skills, and social skills are less developed than many of the other students. He cannot identify most letters. He cannot print his name. He has not spent thousands of hours reading stories with an adult. He colors outside the lines; cannot draw a picture with details like eyes, ears, and hair; and struggles to sit still while listening to the teacher. **During most of the day, standard instruction pushes Bradley into the frustration zone, in which motivation, attention, time-on-task, and learning decline, to be replaced by inattention and acting-out behaviors**.

In some schools there are lots of Bradleys. As the teachers maintain a "rigorous" pace of instruction, these kids fall further behind; establish patterns of disengagement and poor behavior; and start to believe that they are lousy at reading, math, and learning. State and national data clearly shows that poor kids are more likely to be vulnerable to the negative impact of standardized instruction. Young male students (on average) are less developmentally ready for high-pressure standardized instruction in the early grades and have fallen behind females in every category of learning outcome.

In our hearts and minds, we all know what is best for young learners. We know that to maximize learning, help them discover the joy of learning, and to come to see themselves as "good learners," children need lots of success. But our standardized high-pressure, one-size-fits-all systems do not provide high levels of success in the early years to many of our children. The NAEP consistently reports that only about one-third of American students are proficient readers by the beginning of the fourth grade. Only one-fifth of children who are eligible for free or reduced lunch are reading proficiently at this same level. In some poor urban districts, less than one-tenth of the students are proficient in reading and math by the fourth grade. And still the standardized grade-level curriculum gets covered, year after year, to students who do not have the foundational reading, math, behavior, and learning skills needed to succeed.

Consider Detroit, Michigan, and Rochester, New York, as districts with a history of high poverty and poor educational outcomes. The schools in these districts have similar standards for what should be "covered" in each grade-level curriculum. As in every typical school district, a planning process in each district has chosen learning programs and materials which "cover" grade-level content standards. Fourth graders will cover fourth-grade content, using material that is aligned to national standards, written with the assumption that students have learned the previous grade-level content and skills, written with the assumption that students can read, problem solve, and learn with fourth-grade-level skills.

But recent NAEP data suggests a big problem with these assumptions (NCES, 2016). In 2015, 5 percent of students in Detroit performed **at or above** the NAEP Grade 4 Reading Proficient level (4 percent for males, and 7 percent for females). But in a standardized curriculum-driven system, even with 95 percent nonproficient readers, the district continues to rigorously "cover" grade-level material, year after year, somehow pretending that students are not frustrated and disengaged.

It gets worse. The NAEP uses four categories of learner outcomes: Below Basic, Basic, Proficient, and Advanced. Detroit fourth graders were not just slightly behind grade-level proficiency in reading. A majority of students fell into the Below Basic reading category (See Table 5.1). But because they are now in the fourth grade, they will all receive a standard fourth-grade learning program that assumes they already have fourth grade–level skills and understandings.

Table 5.1.   Detroit Fourth Graders Face Reading Frustration

5% Proficient grade-level readers	Experience successful instructional match
21% Basic-level readers	Experience frustrated learning experiences
73% Below basic–level readers	Severe mismatch leading to frustration and disengagement

By design in the CTS educational system, keeping up with the pacing guide is given clear priority over giving kids what they need at their level of readiness. Does anybody think this makes sense?

In a standardized, curriculum-driven, one-size-fits-all instructional system, the first priority is to deliver the standardized grade-level content. In the case of Detroit fourth graders, the standardized language arts content expectations and corresponding learning materials are a mismatch for about 95 percent of the students. Math expectations are a mismatch for 96 percent of students. We can excoriate the teachers and berate the parents all we want, but the systems design for instruction in a district in which so many kids come to school with delayed learning skills is responsible for most of the harm.

Rochester, New York, offers a similar story. Once the home of Kodak, Rochester has fallen on hard economic times. The schools serve families with high rates of poverty and mostly minority students. The New York State English Language Arts (ELA) and math tests are designed to align with NAEP and offer a grades 3 through 8 summary of the percentage of students who are proficient at grade-level standards. Data released by the New York State Department of Education (2016) shows a number of cities in which a large majority of students are nonproficient in both ELA and math, but Rochester claimed the lowest rate of proficiency in the state (See Table 5.2 and 5.3).

Even with overwhelming evidence that their students are struggling, New York school districts continue using a standardized, curriculum-driven,

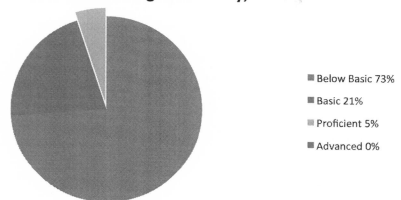

Detroit Fourth-Grade
NAEP Rates of Reading Proficiency, 2015

■ Below Basic 73%

■ Basic 21%

■ Proficient 5%

■ Advanced 0%

Figure 5.1.   Detroit Fourth-Grade Reading Proficiency, National Center for Education Statistics (2016), The Nation's Report Card, 2015 Reading Trial Urban District Snapshot Report Detroit, Grade 4, Public Schools.

Detroit Fourth-Grade
NAEP Rates of Math Proficiency, 2015

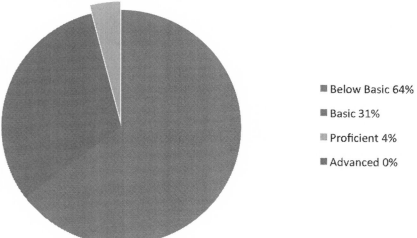

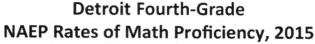

■ Below Basic 64%

■ Basic 31%

■ Proficient 4%

■ Advanced 0%

Figure 5.2.   Detroit Fourth-Grade Math Proficiency, National Center for Education Statistics (2016), The Nation's Report Card, 2015 Math Trial Urban District Snapshot Report Detroit, Grade 4, Public Schools.

Table 5.2. New York School Districts show low rates of proficiency in ELA

Percentage of New York Students Proficient in ELA across All Grades, 3–8

	2015	2016	Percentage Point Change
NYC	30.4	38	7.6
Buffalo	11.9	16.4	4.5
Rochester	4.7	6.7	2
Syracuse	8.1	10.9	2.8
Yonkers	20.3	26	5.7

Table 5.3. New York School Districts show low rates of proficiency in mathematics

Percentage of New York Students Proficient in Math across All Grades 3–8

	2015	2016	Percentage Point Change
NYC	35.2	36.4	1.2
Buffalo	15.1	16.1	1
Rochester	7.4	7.2	−0.2
Syracuse	9.4	10.4	1
Yonkers	24	24.6	0.6

one-size-fits-all instructional system. Fourth-grade students will get fourth-grade content, even if they are significantly behind grade level in reading, even if they lack fundamental math skills and number sense.

> **In the name of rigor and high standards, fourth graders get fourth-grade instruction, ready or not.**

Year after year, grade after grade, class after class, a vast majority of these students are exposed to grade-level content and curricula that will push them into the frustration zone in which motivation, attention, time-on-task, engagement, and learning are diminished. These districts consistently produce poor educational outcomes while using a standardized educational model that is not designed to personalize learning or help a large majority of students become learners for life.

The systems architecture for a competency-based learning design offers a new model for learning. No more one-size-fits-all. A competency-based learning system is designed to embrace neurodiverse learners because neurodiversity is the norm. Such a system is based on far different design specifications that are based on considerably more accurate assumptions about human learning:

- At the same age, all students are not alike in their experiences, rates of development, and learning readiness. Brain diversity is the norm.
- Some students need more time to learn a concept or skill but are fully capable of learning well if given sufficient time.
- All students learn better when offered instruction at a level of challenge that allows for high rates of success.
- Students work better in a community in which they feel safe and connected to others.
- Paying attention to the development of the whole child recognizes the importance of social-emotional intelligence, sensory-motor skills, and also supports academic learning.
- Pushing kids into a frustration zone, in the name of academic rigor, causes students to disengage from learning, stop trying, and even misbehave and disrupt the classroom.
- Pushing vulnerable children into frustration and disengagement from learning is not an acceptable outcome in the age of information and technology advancement.

Giving students what they need, at their correct instructional level, for as long as needed to develop essential skills and learning outcomes is not a radical idea. Moms and dads have used a competency-based system of learning when teaching their kids to walk, throw and catch, ride a bike, learn to swim, cooking, playing games with the family, and just about anything they really want their kids to do well. High-quality coaches, music teachers, karate instructors, dance teachers, and similar teachers of young children certainly do as well. One step at a time, with high rates of success, laughter, and joy, these teachers guide our children to higher levels of skill with patience and respect.

Montessori education is based on a system of guiding children to use learning materials and projects to gradually build higher-level skills. Many early childhood classroom teachers have tried in their own way to offer competency-based learning, although perhaps not always in a systematic way. Teachers of young children have always recognized the variance in language skills, motor skills, and social skills among their students, and have only in recent years been heavily pressured to keep up with rigid pacing guides or follow curriculum in the same way for all students.

Good educators keep coming up with new attempts to use the principles of competency-based learning. In Kennewick, Washington, district staff identified a sequence of skill levels for the development of K–2 language arts skills, including phonemic awareness, phonics, accuracy, fluency, and comprehension. As reported in *Annual Growth for All Students, Catch Up Growth for Those Who Are Behind* (Fielding et al., 2007), progress in these aspects of literacy development was carefully monitored, and students were then given instruction and practice time for each skill until it was mastered. The Kennewick schools were often cited as a model for response to intervention (RTI), which is conceptually a system for providing instruction to match the needs of each student and use systematic measurement of progress to make decisions about adjusting instruction.

Timber Ridge (grades 3–8) and Clover Ridge Schools (K–2), in Albany, Oregon, have implemented standards-based instruction that includes a K–8 scope and sequence, explicit learning objectives, multi-age and subject integration, and a proficiency-based report card.

The Maine School Administrative District 15 has developed learning target maps for the elementary through high school sequence of skills in English-language arts, math, science, social studies, guidance, health-physical education, music, technology and engineering, visual arts, and world language.

Kenowa Hills Public Schools, near Grand Rapids, Michigan, has implemented a competency-based system for K–8 math classes.

Adams County School District 50 began its conversion to standards-based education in 2009. Adams has replaced grades with levels 1–10 that incorporate standards from elementary school through high school graduation. They are developing standards for proficiency, assessment, and improving instruction, and are working with Educate, an instructional technology company, to create an information system to track student progression.

Chugach School District (CSD) serves just over 200 students in a 20,000-square-mile district in south central Alaska. More than 70 percent of students are home-schoolers who are supported through distance learning and fly plane drop-in support. In response to poor outcomes, in 1994 the district began a transition to competency-based learning, and in 2001 CSD was given the prestigious Malcolm Baldrige National Quality Award and in 2009 was selected as a recipient of the APEX Excellence Award. The story of Chugach is well told in *Delivering on the Promise* (2008), by Richard DeLorenzo, Wendy Battino, Rick Schreiber, and Barbara Gaddy-Carrio.

The Early Learning Foundation was established in 2001 and uses *the Essential Skill Inventories, Preschool through Grade 3* (Sornson, 2012a) as a competency framework during the early childhood years. Simpson Central School in rural Mississippi was one of seven pilot districts for the *Essential Skill Inventories*. In 2007–2008, before beginning to use a competency model, 37 percent of Simpson Central third graders scored at proficient or above on the state's reading tests and 59 percent did so in math. In 2013–2014, student outcomes had improved to almost 64 percent in reading and just over 86 percent in math (Sornson and Davis, 2013). At the beginning of the 2014–2015 school year Simpson Central School was rated as a Mississippi "A"- level school, an extraordinary achievement for a high-poverty school.

Rather than focusing on literacy-only skills, the Early Learning Foundation competency frameworks identify a concise set of crucial skills in all the domains of early childhood, including oral language, literacy, phonologic skills, numeracy, sensory-motor skills, behavior, and self-regulation. This reflects the belief that these are interrelated systems, that each domain is crucial for long-term learning success, and is an example of whole-child accountability. While grade-level competencies set the framework for minimum expected outcomes, teachers are also trained to focus on outcomes from a previous grade level or a more advanced level as needed. By systematically updating data on the inventory, teachers become trained to use observational assessment and to embed formative assessment into the design of instruction.

Competency frameworks are not variations on CCSS or any other set of grade-level content standards. Content standards describe what a teacher is expected to "cover." Competency standards describe what students must "learn" with a deep understanding and the ability to apply their skills in multiple ways. Content standards and standards for learning are not the same.

Thoughtful learning standards like those in the Essential Skill Inventories are designed to reflect the developmental sequence of knowledge and skills that lead to higher levels of skill and understanding, one step at a time, with clear descriptions of what proficiency will look like for each learning standard.

Coverage standards can be vague; competencies must be crystal clear.

A growing number of preschool and elementary programs in Michigan, New York, and Mississippi are using the *Essential Skill Inventories* as a PK to grade 3 competency framework. These inventories identify the foundation skills that students must deeply understand and be able to use to allow continued progress toward higher levels of learning. For these skills students will be given instruction at their personal level of readiness for as long as necessary to achieve complete competency. If a student is not ready for a grade-level skill or concept, it may be necessary to step back to a more basic level of learning.

In these schools personalized competency-based learning relies on systematically knowing each student and tracking data weekly on progress toward the essential learning outcomes. Teachers use small groups and center-based learning to thoughtfully differentiate instruction so students can work at their correct instructional level, experience high rates of success, and maintain a growth mind-set. Some students are working on grade-level objectives, while others may be catching up on skills from a previous grade level. When a student demonstrates mastery, it is time to advance to a higher level of challenge. Whole-group instruction is used for projects, exploration, and exposure to interesting concepts and material, but data-based differentiated instruction drives much of the instruction toward the PK to grade 3 essential skills.

In a school that works hard to respect each child's instructional readiness level, behavior problems are fewer. Because the essential skills include movement, oral language, self-regulation, and behavior patterns, teachers are reminded to also focus on these whole child basic needs. Teachers focus more specifically on the needs of each child, and in the process relationships become stronger, based on respect for each child's development and readiness for learning. The focus on social skills reminds teachers to develop play skills, empathy, communication, and self-regulation. Love of learning is specifically built into the learning standards and becomes a partner in the design of instruction.

The golden rule in a competency-based system is to give the child what he or she needs, at his or her level of readiness, for as long as needed.

The Corinth-Alcorn-Prentiss Learning Collaborative in northeast Mississippi tested preschool students using the Star Early Literacy assessment as part of a state-wide assessment process. At the beginning of the 2015–2016 school year, only 20.1 percent of these children scored at or above a standard score of 498, the level associated with readiness for kindergarten entry. Teachers were given training for implementation of the *Preschool Essential Skill Inventory* and asked to use weekly observational assessment to inform instruction to meet the needs of individual students in all the essential skills.

By the end of the year, more than 85 percent of the students showed the literacy skills for K readiness (Sornson, 2015). This pattern of growth gave this collaborative in northeast Mississippi **the highest rate of kindergarten literacy readiness** in the state. Student literacy readiness improved from an average scaled score of 434 in the fall to 597 in the spring, according to the Mississippi Department of Education's Preschool Assessment Result for Early Learning Collaboratives (2016).

The Early Learning Foundation's Five Steps to Competency-Based Learning

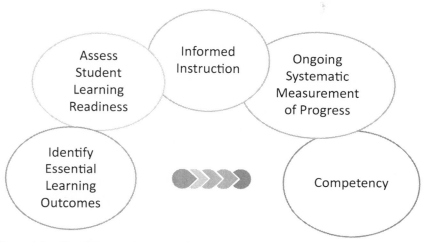

Figure 5.3.   Five Steps to Competency-Based Learning

The *Essential Math Skills Inventory* (Sornson, 2014) is a variation on the *PK to Grade 3 Essential Skills Inventories*. The inventory describes the sequence of twenty-nine math skills that need to be deeply learned from preschool to the third grade, and offers a clear rubric for understanding which students are proficient, developing, or at a level that requires below-grade-level support and intervention. In *Essential Math Skills* (Sornson, 2014) a variety of hands-on or movement-based activities are suggested for each skill. Unlike the one-size-fits-all math learning model, use of the math inventory allows teachers or parents to carefully track progress toward the skills that determine number sense and allow students to progress to higher-level math (appendix A).

As in any application of competency-based learning, teachers are expected to know their students, determine each child's level of instructional readiness, design lessons or choose activities that are engaging and at the correct level of challenge, then monitor progress carefully so that they know which students need more practice to learn a specific skill and which students are ready to move on to higher levels of learning.

It is widely understood that by the end of the third grade we can predict long-term learning outcomes for individual students with astounding accuracy (Annie E. Casey Foundation, 2010; Hernandez, 2011; Sornson, 2012b; Snow et al., 1998; Torgeson, 1998, 2002). Yet in most schools/districts/states there has been no identification of essential learning outcomes, and no system of tracking progress toward the crucial competencies that are the foundation for a lifetime of learning.

Nonetheless, in every state and every community there are thoughtful educators lurking, waiting, and watching for the opportunity to give young students the basic learning and social skills they need. These early years hold the promise of helping every child build a solid foundation for lifelong learning.

Opportunities for Innovation and Entrepreneurship at the Elementary and Preschool Levels:

1. Offer preschools that use specific competency frameworks that allow teachers to know each student's level of readiness within each developmental domain. Use ongoing observational assessment to keep each student's data profile current. Share specific information with parents about their child's development and the learning that is still needed to reach kindergarten readiness. Use data to make decisions about readiness for K placement.
2. Train parents of children in the early childhood years to understand the specific learning and behavior skills that are associated with school success and life success.
3. Experiment with funding models that pay staff a bonus for the number of children who achieve full competency in the early years, or achieve the most growth in the early years.
4. Provide parents who home-school their children a system of tracking progress toward crucial competencies in the early years.
5. Develop and sell play-based and digital learning systems that support progress along the pathway to higher-level competencies in the early years.
6. Allow flexible grouping within elementary schools so that children can receive crucial instruction at the correct instructional level.
7. Coordinate support services (Title 1, Special Education, etc.) so that support teachers have the data to know exactly what each student needs, and their level of readiness for instruction.
8. Offer after-school or tutorial services that interface essential skill data and support instruction focused at student need and instructional readiness.
9. Allow music, art, science, physical education, and other special teachers to access data on student learning needs and support crucial skill development.
10. Develop online support systems for parents who want to learn instructional techniques that match the exact needs of their children.
11. Use in-school innovations like the use of merit badges to track progress from lower- to higher-level skills in all fields of study.

12. Offer mini-classes allowing students to focus on developing a specific skill regardless of age.
13. Assign individual mentor/coaches to work with a child and his or her parents throughout the early years, monitor progress, get to know the child's learning strengths and preferences, and encourage learning beyond the essential learning outcomes in each domain of early childhood development.
14. Develop digital data collection frameworks that offer reminders to teachers, show models of assessment for essential skills, and demonstrations of competency for each essential skill.
15. Develop digital data collection frameworks that provide instructional suggestions to teachers based on class data.

Chapter 6

Personalized Competency-Based Learning in Secondary Schools

Adolescence is the time of great becoming. These years influence how each individual understands himself as a learner and problem-solver, as a social being and citizen. During these years young men and women create a personal identity for themselves in the world, establish habits of behavior, and set a trajectory for self-reliance, responsible behavior, social relationships, and achievement. School is a central part of this adolescent experience, the place in which friends, teachers, classes, sports, music, activities, and social networks become the focus of thinking, dreaming, connecting, and learning.

So what are we really trying to accomplish in the standard American high school? Going back a hundred years or more, this was a much less important question. Schools effectively sorted out the educational winners, and in 1900 only 6 percent of students stayed in school to graduate from high school. These students gathered some general knowledge from their exposure to standard grade-level content and moved into those few jobs that required higher levels of reading and math in the early years of the industrial era.

At the time of the original design of the standard American high school, we did not live in an information age in which lifetime learning and the rapid exchange of ideas were essential for economic and personal success. Now in the 21st century, learning matters for everyone, but still we rely on the one-size-fits-all delivery of standardized curriculum and the use of grades to sort winners and losers. If our goal is to help far more young men and women become effective lifetime learners, the system we are using is antiquated and destructive.

We are failing to help our children develop the learning and problem-solving skills needed to compete in a global marketplace. In a report by the Educational Testing Service (ETS), *America's Skills Challenge: Millennials* *and the Future* (2015), the ETS compared literacy, numeracy, and problem-solving skills of sixteen to thirty-four-year-olds in twenty-two countries using data from the OECD Programme for International Assessment of Adult Competencies. In literacy, U.S. millennials scored lower than fifteen other nations. In both numeracy and problem-solving, U.S. millennials were tied for last.

We are failing to prepare students for advanced level learning. According to *The Reality of College Readiness* (ACT, 2013), only 25 percent of the 1.8 million students taking the ACT exam are college-ready in math, reading, English, and science. More than one-fourth of ACT-tested graduates did not meet any of the four college readiness benchmarks. ACT has defined "college and career readiness" as the acquisition of knowledge and skills a student needs to enroll and succeed in credit-bearing first-year college courses at a postsecondary institution without the need for remediation.

Among students who came from low-income families, whose parents did not go to college, and who identify as black, Hispanic, American Indian, or Pacific Islander, only 9 percent are "strongly ready" for college, which means meeting benchmarks in three of the four readiness areas. By contrast, for students with none of those demographic characteristics, the "strongly ready" rate is six times as high at 54 percent (ACT, 2017). Once again, vulnerable kids are damaged by the standardized one-size-fits-all system.

We are failing to prepare a majority of students for the standards of entry for military service. *Ready, Willing and Unable to Serve* (2009), a report prepared for the joint chiefs of staff, concludes that about 75 percent of the country's seventeen- to twenty-four-year-olds are ineligible for military service, largely because they are poorly educated, are overweight, or have physical ailments that make them unfit for the armed forces. The joint chiefs have called this a national security issue. Those days when the armed services welcomed young men and women with behavior and learning problems are gone.

We are failing to help children of poverty develop the skills to give them an opportunity to succeed in the modern workplace.

- Only 20 percent of fourth-grade children who are eligible for free or reduced lunch are at proficient reading levels (NAEP, 2013).
- In math, only 11 percent of low-income twelfth graders scored at the proficient level (NAEP 2015).
- In reading, only 23 percent of low-income twelfth-grade students scored at the proficient level (NAEP 2015).
- Among African American twelfth-grade students tested, 7 percent are proficient or better in math and only 16 percent are proficient or better in reading (NAEP, 2015).

Brendan is in the tenth grade with a fourth-grade reading level. Because he is in the tenth grade, he will take English 10. Consider the course description for the first semester of this course:

ENGLISH 10A

The first semester of tenth-grade English is a literature survey class. The class covers literary terminology, vocabulary building, test taking strategies, and several literary genres. This semester, we will utilize literature to focus on three central questions: Is there a difference between reality and truth? Can progress be made without conflict? What kind of knowledge changes our lives? The course is written to Common Core Standards and will challenge students to critically think about literature. Students will involve themselves in self-assessment as well as in teacher-guided practice and assessment throughout the class.

The literature of the class includes selections from Nobel Prize in Literature winners and Pulitzer Prize winners. Among the authors and poets included in the class are: Ray Bradbury, W.W. Jacobs, Maya Angelou, Langston Hughes, Sandra Cisneros, Rachel Carson, Anton Chekhov, O. Henry, Leo Tolstoy, Edgar Allen Poe, Rudolfo Anaya, Mark Twain, James Thurber, and Elie Wiesel.

COURSE TOPICS

Students will develop an understanding of: • Theme in fiction • Central ideas in non-fiction • Making predictions • Plot and foreshadowing • Author's perspective • Analyzing structure and format • Comparing style • Cause and effect relationships • Conflict resolution • Author's purpose • Bias of the author or sponsor • Checking the information against reliable sources • Date documents were created/updated • Reliable sources • Character and story structure • Analyzing the text to extend ideas • Comparing points of view • Drawing conclusions about theme • Drawing conclusions about symbolism and allegory • Paraphrasing to connect ideas • Comparing tone • Author's point of view and purpose • Development of ideas • Word choice and tone • Main idea—expository essay • Main idea—reflective essay • Follow and critique technical questions • Comparing humorous writing • Evaluate persuasion arguments and rhetorical devices

With his fourth-grade reading level, every moment of this course will be a challenge for Brendan. While this course is filled with praiseworthy content, it is a terrible mismatch to the needs of this individual student. Brendan has struggled in reading since his earliest years in school. He struggles to read a newspaper or a job application, and this year he will grapple with Chekhov and Tolstoy. These are wonderful authors, whose works might be shared with any good reader at a point in life where they might love the content, but Brendan is not able to read anything included in this course with fluency, deep understanding, or pleasure.

Then, in addition to this completely frustrating English class, let's also give Brendan coursework in chemistry, algebra II, and world history (with a book written at a grade 11 level), and a foreign language, because that is what all tenth graders do.

In some schools more than 90 percent of tenth graders read more like Brendan than a proficient reader. And yet the standards call for all of these students to cover the content standards, keep up with this pacing guide, and take the same test. The learning winners are clearly identified. The losers know who they are, and struggle along in the system that considers one-size-fits-all to be an expression of instructional equity.

Change Gonna Come, Sings Sam Cooke. The days of everybody learns the same content, on the same day, in the same way, are soon to be gone. Our system of taking courses for a passing grade, which does not guarantee that you are proficient in anything, and gathering enough Carnegie credits to graduate from high school, is in the process of being replaced with a systems design that allows students to advance, one step at a time, toward competencies that matter.

In this country, New Hampshire has led the way toward personalized competency-based learning at the secondary level. The state legislature approved new *Minimum Standards for Public School Approval,* under which local districts were required to create standards for competency and begin measuring course credit in these terms by the start of the 2009–2010 school year. The New Hampshire State Board of Education has approved model competency standards for English language arts, mathematics, work study, arts, social studies, and science, but local districts have the autonomy to develop their own standards for competency. Fred Bramante and Rose Colby detailed this transition to CBE in their book *Off the Clock: Moving Education from Time to Competency* (2012).

Maine has also developed a strategic plan for learner-centered instruction, *Education Evolving: Maine's Plan for Putting Learners First* (Maine DOE, 2012). Beginning in 2015, students in Maine were required to demonstrate proficiency in English, math, science, social studies, and health/physical education for graduation.

Iowa, Arizona, Oregon, and Colorado are actively moving toward proficiency-based learning systems. Many other states are developing or studying competency-based systems. Many school districts use blended learning, testing out of courses, or the Khan Academy and other digital learning systems as small steps toward competency-based learning. Virtual schools and online courses use competency-based systems that have varied levels of quality. The use of **micro-credentials** has been incorporated into many technical training programs to demonstrate the specific skills in which each student has become fully proficient.

Competency-based learning systems are an essential part of innovative high school to career initiatives in many parts of the nation. Working with their local high school, and often including a community college partner, employers hope to identify and train local students for skilled and well-paid jobs. Among the many examples are:

- The Advanced Technology Academy and the Advanced Photonic Academy, in Albuquerque, Arizona, are examples. These academies are the focus of collaboration between Sandia National Laboratories, Central New Mexico Community College, and the University of New Mexico.
- The Alamo Area Aerospace Academy (AAAA) is a collaboration of businesses and school in San Antonio, and students spend half the day in high school and the other half learning aerospace maintenance, airframe and power plant mechanics, and other skill sets that may lead to employment or to continued education. In San Antonio, approximately 16 percent of Lockheed Martin's workforce is hired directly from the AAAA.
- Penn Medicine teamed up with schools in the Philadelphia area to create the Penn Medicine High School Pipeline Program. This program enables students from lower socio-economic programs to choose among nursing, allied health care, or nonclinical health care tracks like finance or patient services, and offers incentives for students to enroll in continuing education after high school.
- The Academy for Technology Excellence in Ft. Myers, Florida, was started as collaboration between Dunbar High School and local businesses including Microsoft, Chico's, First Community Bank, and other employers. Serving mostly students from poor households, the program trains students in eighteen computer certifications and other skill areas, offers paid internships, and offers up to forty-eight postsecondary credits.
- Vista High School near San Diego received a $10 million grant from XQ: The Super School Project to scale up its personalized learning system. Vista, located just north of San Diego, piloted this approach with a small group of students enrolled in Vista's Personalized Learning Academy. The

school decided to take this approach school-wide starting with the incoming freshman class in fall 2017.

> **Much of the impetus toward competency-based learning at the secondary level is based on the understanding that students who graduate probably don't have skills that align with the jobs of the present or near future.**

Course credits largely measure seat time, and the recognition that students need skills that matter is not new. In 1991 U.S. secretary of labor Lynn Martin convened the Secretary's Commission on Achieving Necessary Skills (SCANS). Their report described both foundation skills and competencies needed for workplace success. Even though this commission completed its work decades ago, its recommendations are a clear voice for a focus on developing competencies needed for success at work and in life.

Table 6.1. Secretary's Commission on Achieving Necessary Skills (SCANS) Recommendations

SCANS Recommendations, 1991	
COMPETENCIES—effective workers can productively use:	*THE FOUNDATION—competence requires:*
• Resources—allocating time, money, materials, space, and staff • Interpersonal skills—working on teams, teaching others, serving customers, leading, negotiating, and working well with people from culturally diverse backgrounds • Information—acquiring and evaluating data, organizing and maintaining files, interpreting and communicating, and using computers to process information • Systems—understanding social, organizational, and technological systems; monitoring and correcting performance; and designing or improving systems • Technology—selecting equipment and tools, applying technology to specific tasks, and maintaining and troubleshooting technologies	• Basic skills—reading, writing, arithmetic and mathematics, speaking, and listening • Thinking skills—thinking creatively, making decisions, solving problems, seeing things in the mind's eye, knowing how to learn, and reasoning • Personal qualities—individual responsibility, self-esteem, sociability, self-management, and integrity

The European Union has identified key competencies in its *European Framework of Key Competences for Lifelong Learning* (2007). This framework defines eight key competencies and describes the essential knowledge, skills, and attitudes related to each of these. These key competences are communication in the mother tongue, communication in foreign languages, math competence and basic competences in science and technology, digital competence, learning to learn, social and civic competencies, sense of initiative and entrepreneurship, and cultural awareness and expression.

The World Economic Forum's *Future of Jobs Report* (2016) defines ten categories of skill that will support success in the jobs of the future.

An exciting future is waiting for young men and women who have the knowledge and skills identified by the SCANS, or the European Union, or the World Economic Forum, along with self-regulation and empathy, and the willingness to work. Those fortunate enough to love learning, adapting, and collaborating will have incredible opportunities for work, financial success, social success, and interesting lives. Lacking these skills, the future is much less promising. Low-skilled workers will compete for low-paying jobs.

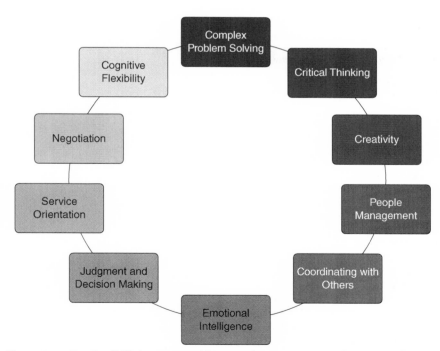

Figure 6.1. Top Ten Skills in 2020 World Economic Forum (2016), The Future of Jobs.

Still, the typical American high school continues to focus on delivering one-size-fits-all instruction toward standardized academic grade-level content objectives. We "cover" a lot of content. We fail to help most of our students become proficient readers and mathematicians, much less develop the other important skills and content our children will need to be successful in the future. And without systems change we will continue to fail the vast majority of our children.

Strong traditions and bureaucratic mandates make these institutions exceedingly difficult to change, but change is upon us.

Opportunities for Innovation and Entrepreneurship at the Secondary Level:

1. Continue to use existing course requirements and credit requirements but allow multiple options for demonstrating the skills associated with each required class. This can start by allowing students to substitute fitness levels demonstrated by participation in a sport for a physical education requirement, or allow specific skills demonstrated in an on-the-job experience for social studies or other credit required for graduation. Allow demonstration of math skills in a robotics or Odyssey of the Mind (a creative problem-solving program) or similar experience for a math credit or specific math requirement. Allow demonstrated skills in a musical for credit in fine arts.

2. Using the New Hampshire, Maine, or other established models, adapt existing high school graduation requirements in your state/district to a competency-based learning structure. This approach establishes exit competencies for high school but does not limit the options that might be considered for reaching these skill levels.

   Progress toward these end goals could be gained through completion of school courses, online courses, free massive open online courses (MOOCs), Khan Academy, internships, sports, starting a business, volunteer work, extracurricular activities, mission trips, making a video, and many other options. Having a clear rubric for the exit-level graduation skills (competencies) is an essential ingredient for this system. Progress toward graduation could be facilitated by a coach/mentor for each student and judged for competency by a review panel. Progress toward graduation could be earned anywhere and at any time.

3. Going beyond one-size-fits-all graduation requirements, and abandoning the typical "course and credit" definition of graduation requirements, a district/state could use the SCANS, European Union, or World Economic

Forum model as the foundation for building a system of skills needed post–high school. But in creating a unique structure, schools could personalize requirements for high school graduation by setting some minimum standards, but also allowing the student to choose some areas of greater interest for additional skill development. For example, musically gifted students could emphasize skills needed for the performing arts; students interested in engineering could emphasize design, math, and science skills; students interested in business could emphasize math for finance, sales skills, oral or written language skills that would support their long-term aspirations.

4. With the opportunity for students to progress toward higher levels of skill while in or outside of school, entrepreneurs could design learning programs and games that do a more effective job of skill development that leads to graduation. Digital games focusing on skill development could be designed to meet students at their exact level of readiness, and challenge them without pushing students into frustration. After-school math, science, or entrepreneurship clubs could track student skill levels and advance them toward personal goals or required outcomes. Online student collaboration forums could house students helping students, and be a source of ideas, projects, and instructional plans.

5. In-school innovations could include the use of merit badges to track progress from lower- to higher-level skills in all fields of study. Educators could offer mini-classes allowing students to focus on developing a specific skill without having to take/retake an entire course. Individual mentor/coaches could develop comprehensive guides for all the options that might be considered when trying to develop a specific set of skills. Student teams could collaborate and support one another in the development and completion of plans that match each individual's learning needs.

Chapter 7

Personalized Competency-Based Learning in Higher Education

Once they were the crown jewels of the American education system. Our universities were admired around the world. Students from other nations competed for admission. And a university degree was the price of admission for prestigious professional jobs and positions of leadership in our communities.

With this history, you might assume that a resistance to change would be toughest in these islands of culture and learning. But in reality, the pace of change toward competency-based learning is faster at our community colleges, colleges, and universities than at any other level of learning in the Unites States. While some schools predictably persist in holding onto old patterns, the move to competency-based learning has begun in hundreds of institutions of higher education.

Driven by the need for degrees that matter, questions about the efficacy of many college degrees, and concerns over cost and poor completion rates, there are colleges, universities, community colleges, technical schools, and certification programs in every corner of the nation that are offering competency-based learning options. In these innovative programs learners may be given credit for skills learned on the job, in another institution, or independently. Progress can be made at an individual's rate of learning. Competency might be demonstrated by performance-based assessment, using projects that demonstrate both knowledge and application, or by portfolio. CBL transcripts can include much more than just a list of courses taken, detailing the specific skills and accomplishments demonstrated by the learner over time.

In this quickly evolving arena, here are some of the leading stories of competency-based learning in action:

- Western Governors University was chartered in 1996, supported by the Western Governors Association, to use competencies rather than seat time as the measure of its outcomes, and to take advantage of distance learning opportunities. It has grown to become an accredited national university, with more than 50,000 students in all fifty states, offering competency-based degrees at the associate, bachelor, and master's levels.

- At DePaul University's School for New Learning, students earn degrees by demonstrating the competencies required for the degree. They can take courses that are related to those competencies or develop portfolios that demonstrate mastery of those competencies through prior learning. Some coursework is required.
- Excelsior College School of Nursing has offered an accredited competency-based associates degree for almost four decades. The program is designed for students transitioning from a licensed practical nurse to a registered nurse role, or coming to nursing with a clinical background. Students complete general education requirements through coursework, must successfully demonstrate nursing clinical skills, and pass a computer simulation examination measuring clinical competence.
- Capella University's FlexPath allows students to complete as many courses per quarter as they can for one flat tuition rate in the departments of business, information technology, and psychology. The university allows students to receive credit for knowledge already gained through their experience with a "prior learning assessment."
- The University of Wisconsin offers its Flexible Option, comprised of five competency-based online programs leading to a certificate or bachelor's degree.
- Purdue University offers a transdisciplinary bachelor's degree program based on learned and demonstrated competencies at the Purdue Polytechnic Institute and the College of Technology.
- The University of Michigan offers a competency-based master's degree program for IHE (Institutes of Higher Education) health profession educators. The program prepares practicing professionals in medicine, nursing, dentistry, pharmacy, public health, social work, and other health professions to become health profession educators. MPHE students choose from among twenty-one competencies that are tied to various health professions. Each enrolling student's experience and previous learning is reviewed by a competency assessment panel, and then assigned credit for existing competencies. Students are assigned a mentor, and an individualized program is designed to meet the needs of each student.
- In partnership with 2U, Simmons College offers graduate competency-based online programs in nursing and social work.
- Southern New Hampshire University offers competency-based programs (health care management, communications, general studies, and management) to federal employees through College of America.

- At Arizona State University the open-access Global Freshman Academy allows students to pay when they successfully complete courses.
- Northern Arizona University offers a competency-based online learning program that allows students to use their previous experience to pass pre-tests. The program offers bachelor's degrees in computer information technology, liberal arts, and small business administration, and it is accredited by the Higher Learning Commission of the North Central Association of Colleges and Schools.
- The American Public University, with enrollment at 90,000, offers four competency-based undergraduate degrees that require students to master at least sixty competency-based modules for completion, and eliminates the credit hour standard.
- The Lumina Foundation developed the Degree Qualifications Profile (DQP) to provide a baseline set of reference points for what students should know and be able to do to earn an associate's, bachelor's, and master's degree. The DQP defines educational outcomes in terms of what graduates know and can do in the areas of applied learning, intellectual skills, specialized knowledge, broad knowledge, and civic learning. The Western Association of Schools and Colleges, the Higher Learning Commission, the Southern Association of Colleges and Schools, the Council of Independent Colleges and Universities, and several universities are working with the Lumina Foundation to test and further develop the DQP.
- The Global Learning Qualifications Profile (GLQP) was developed by Open SUNY, based in part on the LEAP project's essential learning outcomes and rubrics. The GLQP emphasizes assessment of college-level outcomes obtained through open learning sources, including Open Educational Resources (OERs), MOOCs, and prior or experiential learning.

Competency-based learning in higher education is taking advantage of some of the obvious inefficiencies of the traditional course and credit system. Instead of measuring seat time, these programs are tracking the development of real skills, skills that matter, and/or skills that align with the jobs available in a community. Instead of requiring three hours of work per week (one hour of lecture and two hours of study) over a minimum of sixteen weeks to earn one college credit, clearly defined learning outcomes can be completed in as little or as much time as needed.

Some programs offer **micro-credentials**, like merit badges, which can be earned one step at a time, and that lead to a set of desired skills. Some programs offer training to achieve a degree or certification, and then ongoing access to learning options throughout your professional career. Learning is now for life, and some institutions of higher learning are leading the way. They are determined to be available to meet the learning needs of students throughout the many phases of a career and in response to the different scenarios for individual learning that are emerging in a world of ever-changing technology and innovation.

As quickly as competency-based higher education is developing, there are bound to be some programs that take shortcuts, cut costs, or offer faux competency-based learning systems. Buyer beware.

In the appendix is a complete rubric for considering the quality of IHE competency-based learning initiatives. With five levels, the highest level of quality among competency-based learning systems can be judged using this rubric. See Appendix B for the complete rubric, which includes five levels of quality.

Quality of Higher Education Competency-Based Learning Initiatives, Level 5

- **Minimum competencies are clearly established for a certificate or degree, including knowledge, skill, and application**
- **Additional learning goals are established based on the individual needs and interests of the student**
- **A review/assessment of knowledge, skill, and application helps determine each student's learning needs within the program**
- **A review/assessment of the student's learning strengths and style helps contribute to the development of a personalized learning plan**
- **Personalized learning plans focus on achievement of the required competencies and the student's chosen goals**
- **Specific short-term learning plans are developed by the facilitator and student, and can include specific modules, learning materials, or experiences**
- **Cohort groups, online networks, or other support group structures are available**
- **Students receive frequent and systematic assessment of progress**
- **Timely instructional support is available**
- **Students advance upon demonstrated mastery of learning goals leading to required competencies and student-initiated learning goals**
- **Degree or certificate is awarded upon demonstration of all required competencies**

College, university, and certificate programs that earn a reputation for offering training that lead to high-quality skills that matter, efficient use of time and resources, and respecting the different learning needs of their students will likely succeed at levels never seen before. Learning is not just local anymore. High-quality training/learning systems will attract learners from around the world.

Opportunities for Innovation and Entrepreneurship at the Higher Education Level:

1. Replace seat time requirements for select courses with clear minimum standards for learning and application of knowledge. Coverage standards can be vague, but competencies must be crystal clear.
2. Replace seat time and course requirements for select certifications and degrees with clear minimum standards for learning and application of knowledge.
3. Develop a portfolio of ways students might demonstrate competency for specific learning goals.
4. Allow students to choose some required learning goals in which they want to exceed minimum standards, and personalize the learning process to help students meet these higher levels of expectation.
5. Create a process for assessing student learning experiences and existing skill levels, allowing student learning to begin at their level of readiness.
6. Train existing or new staff to serve as "coaches/mentors" for students, supporting the development of personalized learning plans and then supporting students as they reach each step in the progression of earning certificates or degrees.
7. Develop a process for using cohort groups, online or in person, to support the review of student plans for learning, plans for demonstration of competency, and submissions to demonstrate proficiency as part of an individual's personal learning plan.
8. Ask students to develop a personal vision for learning as an initial step in the development of personalized learning plans.
9. Develop check-in and feedback systems to give students quality and timely feedback as they continue to work their way toward their personal learning goals.
10. Build a transcript system that reflects student skills and accomplishments, with an emphasis on having an in-depth summary of each student's achieved skill levels.
11. Develop a system that uses established "experts," still working or retired, to support the students' progress in their personalized learning plans.
12. Develop a menu of "mini-classes" that would address a small set of learning goals, and could appeal to students in any competency-based learning system.
13. Find companies in your community with an interest in developing students with a skill set that would allow them to be good candidates for

employment in high-skill positions. Allow these companies to help set criteria needed for employment, to allow staff members to serve as mentors, and to provide internships.

14. Develop a micro-credential or merit badges system that can be used to track student learning accomplishments throughout a professional career or throughout life.

Chapter 8

How to Suck Innovation Out of the American Education System

We live in an era of transformation. In science and industry we witness scientific inquiry, information, technology, and the capacity for change. In the past few decades change has become the constant, affecting every aspect of the way we live and work. Satellites roam our skies, bringing us information and entertainment. We talk to our phones, and they guide us turn by turn as we travel. The smartphone in your pocket has more computing power than the entire National Aeronautics and Space Administration (NASA) when astronauts completed the moon mission. We can search for information on any topic with astonishing speed. Diseases that once ravaged the planet have been eliminated or diminished. Many of us safely travel tens of thousands of miles through the air each year. We've mapped the human genome and discovered the human microbiome.

And then there are schools. Still teaching a one-size-fits-all curriculum to all kids of the same age. Still racing through content whether students are interested or capable of success. Still teaching biology before chemistry and physics because that's the alphabetic order. Still taking summer off so kids can help in the fields. Still providing better funding to schools in higher-income communities. Still paying teachers more for years served but not for effectiveness.

We have successfully sucked innovation out of the American education system. Let's consider the factors that support our stagnation.

THE PRIMARY INNOVATION KILLER: THE DESIGN OF PUBLIC EDUCATION ITSELF

In 1843 Horace Mann, as secretary to the first Massachusetts State Board of Education, traveled to Europe to choose a system for the first American

59

public schools. He chose the Prussian system, which offered an eight-year course of primary education and emphasized the skills needed in an early industrialized world (basic reading, writing, and arithmetic) along with education in ethics, duty, discipline, and obedience. This became the system adopted by other states.

Most students were not expected to stay in school for long, often just a few months or a few years. The standard grade-level learning materials used in schools were limited by cost and availability. By the turn of the century grades 9 through 12 had been added to the system, but nationally only 6.4 percent of students chose to stay in school and graduate from high school. This rate of high school completion was sufficient to meet the needs for educated teachers and other professionals, while most people saw no need for high-level academic skills in their lives. The system worked well to meet the needs of society at that time because there was no pressure for all students to succeed in school.

During the early 1900s, Frederick Winslow Taylor stamped his mark on public education. As one of the first management consultants, and as a leader of the Efficiency Movement, Taylor was an advocate of scientific management, which looked for the most efficient way to accomplish a task. This was described as "the one best way." Taylor recommended enforced standardization of methods, a clear distinction between management and workers, and strong management control (Kanigel, 1997).

The development of curriculum, grade-level learning material, and standard delivery of instruction reflect the philosophy of Taylor. Students were organized into classrooms by grades, in spite of what we see today as significant variance among the learning readiness of same-age students. Instruction was organized into subject areas, separating social studies from reading, math from science. Standard units of time (class periods) were used to separate subject areas and give the same time to each subject. Teachers were separated into classrooms designed for teacher-directed coverage of grade-level curricula. The distinction between teaching staff and administration was clearly delineated, and reinforced by pay, power, and prestige.

Taylor's influence on the design of our schools has persisted over time. We still separate kids by grade, cover standardized curricula by subject matter, create pacing guides to keep teachers on track, offer credits by measuring seat time, and confer graduation diplomas that measure the number of credits rather than the learning skills of our students. Students are subjected to "the one best way" of standardized instruction, which is incredibly boring for some and frustrating and impossible for others.

After World War II, interest in improved learning outcomes increased, and high school graduation and college entry rates began to rise significantly. Many more people saw education as important for their own lives, and for the lives of their children. But as the perceived importance of education increased, we held onto our familiar model of instruction: efficient delivery of a standard curriculum. Cover the material, test the students, and move on to the next unit of instruction.

During the 1970s and 1980s, international competition and the need for better-trained workers stirred more calls for education reform. We responded to the pressure for better outcomes by speeding up the assembly line. We added more content, much more. Teachers are now expected to cover an impossible body of content in the time allotted. We shifted some of this content to earlier grades, which means that content once delivered in the fourth grade may now be covered in the second grade. We added testing systems to hold teachers and schools accountable.

Education in modern schools has become a frantic race to cover and test the students. The system we use today is still based on an 1840s design for instruction. We've accelerated the rate of coverage and turned teachers into thoughtless minions by asking them to follow the "one best way" of instruction. We cover content whether students are ready or not. We test students and label them winners and losers. And then we move on to the next unit so that we can keep up with the prescribed pacing guide.

Somehow we've clung to the idea that covering more using *the one best way* of standardized instruction, covering faster, adding high-stakes standardized assessments, pressuring students, pressuring teachers, and pressuring administrators would lead to better learning outcomes when there is no valid research to support these beliefs.

STANDARDIZED ONE-SIZE-FITS-ALL INSTRUCTION

As a parent, coach, music teacher, or karate instructor, good teaching involves knowing your students and offering instruction that is matched to their personal readiness level, challenging but not overwhelming. Building relationships with students, knowing their personal interests and learning styles, and developing routines for learning can also support the process of getting kids to learn and fall in love with learning.

But in recent decades, we have morphed Taylor's *one best way* of instruction into a system that strips all professionalism from the teacher. State or national content standards define what should be "covered." Textbooks and learning programs define the lessons that will be presented to cover the required content. District-provided pacing guides define the pace at which instruction will be offered **to all students**. District or nationally standardized assessment systems add pressure to make teachers keep up with the prescribed pace of coverage.

Ask any teacher. They know which kids are struggling. While teachers may not have a specific framework for understanding which underlying skills are poorly developed and restricting a student's ability to keep moving forward within a domain of learning, they do know which students can't keep up no matter how hard they may try. And yet the district requires that they keep up the pace of instruction, keep covering lessons, giving tests, moving on even while the frustration builds up within these students.

Inexplicably assuming that all students should be at the same level of instructional readiness, mindlessly accepting that all students in a grade or course are ready for the same lesson on the same day, and cruelly punishing kids who cannot keep up with poor grades and assignment to the Learning Losers category is a form of inhumanity that must stop. The system we've constructed treats teachers like idiots while it damages a majority of our students.

A SCHOOL CULTURE OF FEAR AND CONFORMITY

The Taylorian model of the "one best way" of instruction included standardized curriculum and firm lines of authority from the top down, from state to local, from principal to teacher, and from teacher to student. In recent decades we've put this authoritarian model on steroids, stripped teachers and students of almost all decision making, and created a culture of one-size-fits-all conformity that even Taylor never imagined.

The best definition of an organization's culture is: The way things really work around here.

- Do members of the organization consistently work to build positive professional relationships?
- Is positivity in action and communication the accepted norm on the job?
- Is innovation encouraged, or are staff members afraid to try something new or different?
- Do members read, get together to brainstorm new ideas, collaborate to expand their thinking, and develop personally meaningful professional goals?
- Are staff engaged in constantly trying to make the system work even better?

Successful organizations typically have a culture of learning, collaboration, positive communication, and trust. Many teachers and administrators have reported leaving the profession because there is just not much joy anymore, and because the culture of schools has become negative, fear-driven, and anxious. Many bright young men and women reject the possibility of becoming a teacher because of the perceived negativity, the lack of appreciation, and respect for teachers in American public schools.

> **Teachers are not treated as professionals when they are told exactly what all kids in their grade need to learn, given teaching programs that are delivered to all kids in the same way, and given pacing guides and district assessments which further coerce compliance with the demands of coverage.**

We've created a system of "Teaching for Dummies." In their edicts and regulations, legislators and departments of education have clearly implied that teachers are not allowed to personalize education to the needs or interests of students, not capable of finding a better way than the standardized process, and must not allow their own personalities to influence the way in which content is explored in their classrooms.

We've created an organizational system built on fear and compliance. The states are afraid of the feds. The school districts are terrified of the state. The schools are petrified of the district. The teachers are intimidated by principal mandates. The students, at the end of this fear-based daisy chain, go to school in a culture built upon intimidation and control.

LACK OF COMMITMENT TO PROFESSIONAL LEARNING

We live in the heyday of the learning organization. Start-up companies strive to be ahead of the curve, developing new ideas or technology, or finding ways to use existing systems in new and more effective ways. More than half a million new businesses get started in the United States each month, and these are responsible for almost all the new jobs created within our economy. It is a time of learning and change. We live in a world where half of the jobs of today won't exist tomorrow and where half of the jobs of tomorrow don't exist yet today.

Schools are the traditional centers for learning within a community. As such, you might assume that adults working within schools are themselves continuous learners, excited about learning, looking for new ideas, collaborating and sharing new ideas with others, always looking to expand their opportunities to learn so that they can improve their own lives and the lives of their students. That assumption would be wrong.

Most schools are the antithesis of a learning organization, holding onto old patterns in the face of change. We grant teaching certificates to candidates who have accumulated enough seat time to be awarded enough "credits," which may or may not be associated with the knowledge and skills needed to become a teacher.

No states at this writing have a set of competencies that must be demonstrated to become a teacher. Instead we have lists of content objectives that must be "covered" within the courses required for a teaching degree.

Continuing education units measure seat time in a lecture, training, or meeting, and sufficient seat time allows educators to maintain their ongoing certification.

Committees study which one-size-fits-all program to buy as a replacement of the last one-size-fits-all program that failed to improve test scores, and work diligently to create pacing guides that will allow teachers to cover all the lessons in the time available.

Professional development time is allocated to carefully study new legal challenges and new U.S. Department of Education and state regulations, which keeps us legal as we continue to offer the same basic design for instruction we had in the 1850s and the 1950s.

PLCs (Professional Learning Communities) are ubiquitous in the world of schools but usually lack focus on improving specific student learning outcomes, and few PLCs achieve the drastically improved results that are the whole purpose for having them.

Peter Senge (1994) asserts, "The rationale for any strategy for building a learning organization revolves around the premise that such organizations will produce dramatically improved results." But national data clearly shows an absence of any significant improvement in education outcomes since we first began using the National Assessment of Educational Progress in the early 1970s. Schools are the quintessential holdouts in a world of learning and change.

USE OF THE EXPERT MODEL TO ISOLATE CONSUMERS FROM THE DECISION-MAKING PROCESS

Parents may be over-involved with the wrong things in some schools, like the selection of band uniforms, writing papers for their children, arguing with teachers over grades, and the details of eighth-grade graduation. But the delivery of standardized one-size-fits-all instruction preempts parent involvement with decisions that are crucial for the success of their children.

How many schools ask parents to carefully describe what they know about a child's learning interests, or to describe their daughter's/son's academic and social learning needs, or to collaborate in achieving individual learning goals?

To the CTS education model, such questions are sweet but irrelevant. Fifth grade is going to cover fifth-grade content standards using the (*blank*) language arts, math, science, or social studies instructional program, regardless of your child's precious learning preferences and needs.

The standards we "cover" were determined by a group of experts selected by the National Governors Association (NGA) and the Council of Chief State School Officers (CCSSO). Our learning programs, research- and evidence-based of course, were chosen by a district committee. Our district has high expectations and rigorous curricula, and our instructional program is based on best practice. We know what's best. Drop off your kids, and we'll take it from there.

PROTECT MEDIOCRITY

In some states poor pay limits the quality of candidates for the teaching profession. South Dakota, Mississippi, and Oklahoma lead the way with poor pay, with average 2015–2016 teaching salaries below $45,000. According to a study by the National Association of Colleges and Employers, the teaching profession has an average national starting salary of $30,377. Meanwhile, NACE finds that other college graduates who enter fields requiring similar training and responsibilities start at higher salaries. Computer programmers start at an average of $43,635, public accounting professionals at $44,668, and registered nurses at $45,570. Not only do teachers start lower than other professionals, but the more years they put into teaching, the wider the gap gets. One sign of the impact is that only 5 percent of the students in a recent survey of college-bound students were interested in pursuing a career in education, a decrease of 16 percent between 2010 and 2014.

New York City's famous "rubber rooms" or reassignment centers are one example of how hard it can be to fire teachers charged with misconduct or incompetence. These are the rooms where an estimated 200 to 400 teachers get paid while awaiting disciplinary hearings, and where they spend six hours and twenty minutes, day after day, sometimes for years. This is just one egregious example of a pattern that holds true in most public schools across the nation. Teachers like the safety of tenure and union contract protections. Staff members who are well known for incompetence are somehow protected and indeed rewarded by the system of giving more pay for seniority.

For many bright college students it is the frustrating working conditions, bureaucratic requirements, lack of opportunity for growth, and the lack of public respect and appreciation for teachers that keeps them away from the education profession. Among the most successful international education systems it is well accepted that attracting and keeping the best candidates is crucial for building a highly successful design for learning. As competency-based learning systems grow and replace CTS instructional models, the need for teachers who can learn, problem-solve, innovate, and collaborate will only increase.

> **But for now, we don't pay teachers enough, we don't fire teachers enough, and we don't use a systems design that attracts a sufficient number of new educators who are world-changers.**

THE STRANGLEHOLD OF BUREAUCRATIC REGULATIONS

Good teachers are more abundant in schools with good cultures. Good school culture typically grows out of good leadership. Successful teaching and good school cultures don't have an exact formula, but they do have a necessary condition. **Teachers and administrators must have the freedom to use their training, experience, and best instincts to respond to the needs of students. They must recognize the unique needs of students individually and collectively, and use every talent they have to meet those needs.**

But our schools are designed to cover content, not to ensure that each student learns. In the early 1900s the delivery of standardized content was influenced by Taylor's *one best way*, and schools entered the era of standardized delivery of standardized content. Over time we developed state and local education bureaucracies, which began to develop volumes of regulations to refine and control standardized delivery of one-size-fits-all instruction. And then the process of regulation was put on steroids by NCLB.

> **If you're going to sin, sin against God, not the bureaucracy. God will forgive you, but the bureaucracy won't.**
>
> **—Admiral Hyman G. Rickover**

The greatest shift toward federalism in the history of American public education took place in 2001, and it happened with relatively little public debate or scrutiny by the media and educational organizations. No Child Left Behind's first goal was to eliminate achievement gaps between subgroups among American public school students. Boys and girls and children of all races would achieve learning success at similar levels, which would be carefully monitored by state assessment tests. NCLB's second promise was that all American students would reach proficiency in reading and math by 2014. How could anyone argue with such persuasive goals? Certainly, the federal government was about to get it right.

But more regulations, more identification of failing schools, more sanctions, more pressure, and more testing did not change the underlying design or the outcomes of a one-size-fits-all education model.

District efforts to avoid NCLB sanctions by showing annual yearly progress in every subgroup on the annual state standardized achievement tests have driven many school administrations to absurd responses. Many schools have narrowed their curricula, cutting art, music, physical education, and recess, all in the hope of higher scores in the tested subjects. Lesson plans must include every CCSS standard to be covered this week. Daily standards must be written on the classroom whiteboard. Administrators evaluate whether teachers are keeping up with the pacing guide, covering the correct standards of the day, preparing kids for the district assessment that prepares kids for the state assessment, with the weird assumption that covering all the content expectations for all kids at the same time will improve student learning which will then improve the test scores.

Districts discard last season's one-size-fits-all teaching program for another version that claims to be better aligned to the grade-level coverage standards. When this strategy does not work, the bureaucracy demands more coverage, more testing, more rules, and more rigidity. Regulations are everywhere in schools. Teachers and principals spend hours every week filling out forms that no one ever reads. Many teachers have learned to tolerate misbehavior rather than running the risk of a due process hearing. Administrators struggle to meet state regulations while balancing work rules developed as part of union contracts.

Teachers are treated like cogs in the one-size-fits-all system that has been created by bureaucratic responses to a political, legal, and media frenzy. NCLB and every other recent federal initiatives have contributed to the over-regulation of our schools and the demoralization of American educators. State and federal bureaucrats are sure they know better, and so they devise complex regulations and penalties. Educators are caught in senseless, disorienting, and menacingly complex Kafkaesque bureaucracies. This is not what they signed up for when they heeded the call to become a teacher.

HAND CONTROL OF PUBLIC EDUCATION TO BUREAUCRATS AND POLITICIANS

In 1983 the President's Commission on Excellence in Education published its report, *A Nation at Risk: The Imperative for Educational Reform*. The report famously stated, "The educational foundations of our society are presently being eroded by a rising tide of mediocrity that threatens our very future as a Nation and a people. If an unfriendly foreign power had attempted to impose on America the mediocre educational performance that exists today, we might well have viewed it as an act of war." The report supported the idea that American schools were failing and touched off a wave of state and federal reform efforts that continue to this day.

In 1989 President George H. W. Bush convened a summit with governors, business leaders, and key political advisors in Charlottesville, Virginia, for the first ever National Education Summit. Bill Clinton (Arkansas), Roy Romer (Colorado), and Terry Branstad (Iowa) were key leaders among the governors. **No educators were invited to this summit, which laid the foundation for federal education policy for years to come**.

The summit led to Goals 2000: Educate America Act (March 1994), which famously promised that by the year 2000:

1. Every child will start school ready to learn.
2. The high school graduation rate will increase to at least 90 percent.
3. American students will leave grades 4, 8, and 12 having demonstrated competency over challenging subject matter including English, mathematics, science, foreign languages, civics and government, economics, art, history, and geography; and every school in America will ensure that all students learn to use their minds well, so they may be prepared for responsible citizenship, further learning, and productive employment in our nation's modern economy.
4. The nation's teaching force will have access to programs for the continued improvement of their professional skills needed to instruct and prepare all American students for the next century.
5. U.S. students will be first in the world in science and mathematics achievement.
6. Every adult American will be literate and will possess the knowledge and skills necessary to compete in a global economy and exercise rights and responsibilities of citizenship.
7. Every school in the United States will be free of drugs, violence, and the unauthorized presence of firearms and alcohol and will offer a disciplined environment conducive to learning.

8. Every school will promote partnerships that will increase parental involvement and participation in promoting the social, emotional, and academic growth of children.

The 1989 Bush Education Summit, Goals 2000, NCLB, CCSS, Race to the Top, ESEA waivers, and the Every Student Succeeds Act (ESSA) are rooted in the same political soil, based on the belief that legislative action and Department of Education regulations could improve education outcomes. But the glorious promises of Goals 2000 have not been realized.

The empty words of politicians, in combination with the brute force of federal and state regulators, have led to unimproved national learning outcomes and a general apathy among voters who no longer believe in the efficacy of school reform. Schools have less time for relationships, joy, nature, and art as they unproductively chase content coverage and test scores. And frustrated educators are prevented from serving the individual needs of their students as they submissively pursue keeping up with the pacing guide.

> **Every revolution evaporates and leaves behind only the slime of a new bureaucracy.**
>
> — **Franz Kafka**

Basically, in most modern K–12 schools the bureaucrats are in charge. In the name of standardized "one best way" instruction, we consistently use practices that are clearly at odds with the heart of what we know about learning and teaching.

TEACH TO THE TEST AND MAKE TEACHING AND LEARNING A RACE

In the first century of American public schools, we used a low-pressure version of standardized instruction. After World War II, the pressure gently increased, then accelerated with the advent of school reform in the 1980s and 1990s. In recent years the pressure is full bore and unabated.

State and national content coverage standards. Federally required annual standardized assessment. Pacing guides. Scripted learning programs. District assessment systems. Third-grade retention legislation. Curriculum alignment to the content coverage standards. Failing schools. Teacher evaluation

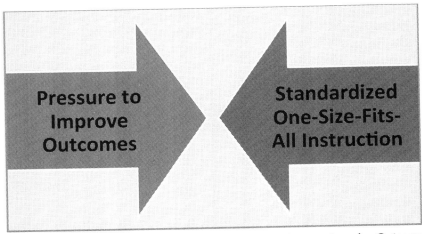

Figure 8.1.   Standardized Instruction Stymies Pressure to Improve Learning Outcomes

systems. Teacher evaluation based on student test scores. Ranking schools. Failing schools based on a single subgroup. School report cards.

So much pressure and so few results. Decades of school reform have failed to achieve any significant improvement in U.S. student learning outcomes.

Administrators, teachers, and students are engaged in an unhappy and fruitless race to cover grade-level content, teach to the tests, take the tests, and blame someone else for the unfortunate outcomes. Teacher job satisfaction is low, and we are not attracting the best candidates to enter our profession. The pressure is palpable. To students, school feels more like prison than ever. We grind through the content standards at an unholy pace, with less time for relationships, social-emotional learning, character development, play, exploration, and discovering personal learning interests.

For decades, educators have been aware that they are racing through content without achieving a deep understanding or the ability to apply learning for a vast majority of their students. In a comparison of U.S. curricula to that of high-achieving countries (Schmidt et al., 2001, 2005; Schmidt and Cogan, 2009), the number of science and math topics covered in U.S. school is significantly greater, and the amount of repetition of content from grade to grade is almost double that of the better-achieving school systems.

In 1999 Schmoker and Marzano advised educators, "We will realize the promise of school reform when we establish standards and expectations for reaching them that are clear, not confusing; essential, not exhaustive. The result will be a new coherence and a shared focus that could be the most propitious step we can take toward educating all students well."

In 2008 the National Council of Teachers of Mathematics recommended that "math curriculum should include fewer topics, spending enough time to make sure each is learned in enough depth that it need not be revisited in later grades. That is the approach used in most top-performing nations." In 2009 John Hattie urged us to *clarify what students must learn* as the first step for a successful learning strategy.

In spite of consistent recommendations to slow down the pace of instruction, there is little evidence that anyone is listening. In recent years, the narrative to the Common Core State Standards calls us to cover fewer topics to a deeper level of understanding so that topics do not need to be retaught in subsequent grades. But the fear of not being ready for the mandated state and national tests seems to have limited our ability to respond thoughtfully and truly narrow the scope of instructional content.

When teaching a young child to throw and catch, we refuse to follow a pacing guide. Instead we take the time to play, ensure high rates of success, and gradually increase challenge without causing frustration and disengagement. When teaching a teenager to drive a car, wise parents take all the necessary time to practice driving in the school parking lot before moving to the side roads, and all the time needed on the side roads before moving to the main roads, and all the time needed on main roads before moving to the expressways, and all the time needed driving during good weather conditions until allowing your child to drive in more difficult weather.

But in most schools, despite the clear importance of helping kids love to learn and become good learners for life, we charge ahead with our cover-test-sort standardized one-size-fits-all methodology in the face of every reason.

In the 21st century, good teachers are being asked to use the supercharged version of a curriculum-driven instructional model that treats kids as if they were learning on an assembly line. Covering way too much content at an unreasonable rate, with rigid pacing guides that make it impossible to find time to shape instruction to meet the individual needs of students, the system is breaking down. In spite of teaching to the test, our children are not doing better on international comparisons or compared to previous decades. Good teachers are discouraged. Many of the best and brightest college students cannot imagine subjecting themselves to working in such a broken system.

When it comes to human learning, quantity does not equate to quality. Our curriculum-driven instructional model, on steroids since the advent of national school reform initiatives, has consistently failed to help more students love learning, or to attain high levels of skill in literacy, numeracy, or problem-solving. Poor children are especially vulnerable to the adverse effects of this model, but all of students suffer from our continued reliance on this design for teaching and learning.

AVOID DEALING WITH INCONVENIENT TRUTHS

At the district, school, and classroom levels we have reached an all-time low level of innovation. We are afraid. For decades we've been told what to cover, at what pace, how to teach, what to test, and how to test. Many educators are even afraid to speak up, to describe the obvious truths that they observe in their classrooms and in their schools. **Here are a few of the elephants (inconvenient truths) in the room:**

- We taught it, but they didn't learn it.
- Half my class is not ready for some of the grade-level prescribed curriculum.
- Billy is tired and hungry. His clothes are dirty and he cries a lot. He is not able to plow through the curriculum today. He needs something else.
- Instead of covering twenty to thirty content standards today, my kids need to work on self-calming, focusing, persisting, delaying gratification, and learning to play nicely with each other.
- Behaviors are out of control, in part because I no longer have the time to build relationships and teach appropriate school behaviors and routines.
- Some kids don't give a darn about the test, don't try hard, and the test results are a poor reflection of their learning.
- We spend so much time on test preparation that I have much less time available for real teaching and learning.
- Covering tenth-grade math content with a group of poor kids who do not have basic number sense that they should have learned in K–3 is an impossible task.
- Using science books with a twelfth-grade reading level with kids who are below sixth-grade reading level is unfair to those kids.
- My students are less intrinsically motivated to learn than they were many years ago when we covered less and had more time for class projects.
- Kids are coming into class with lower levels of readiness, and yet the district expects us to teach more challenging content at younger ages.
- I covered the unit. Three kids already understood the content before I began to teach it, but most of my students passed the unit test with less than 80 percent correct. Some of my students really didn't learn anything because they don't have the foundation skills for that unit. Tomorrow I'll start another unit. I guess the pattern will repeat.
- My students mostly do what they are told, but they do not love to learn.
- Students are afraid to make mistakes, avoid admitting mistakes, and don't learn from them.
- New teachers need a far more careful induction into the profession than they get in most schools.

- Our school has a PLC, but we have never focused on the first critical question: *What do we expect students to learn?* Focusing on getting better test scores, or finding a better correlated math program, is not the same thing.
- At the beginning of the year we begin teaching without ever seriously assessing the learning needs and readiness of our students. We just charge ahead into the curriculum.
- I am teaching sixth-grade math, but I don't understand much about the foundation skills students need to be successful in my class.
- I know which kids are struggling in my class, but other than nurturing and encouraging them, there is not much I can do to help.
- No rational adult would throw a small hard ball at a child who is not fully able to catch it. Why then does math instruction in most schools consistently throw hardballs at kids who aren't ready?
- By the third grade the kids have clearly sorted themselves into learning winners and learning losers. That is so wrong, but we continue to produce the same outcome.
- I give grades based on how kids score on a Bell Curve, but a B or a C seldom means that students have achieved a deep understanding of the content.
- The learning outcomes of our students do not align well with the SCANS or EU or any other set of outcomes needed for good employment in the 21st century.
- Economically disadvantaged and minority kids are more likely to fall behind grade-level expectations, and yet we continue to push them forward into the next unit or the next grade without many of the foundation skills and knowledge needed to succeed.
- The divide between the rich and the poor is growing in our country. But we are failing to give many kids the self-regulation skills, social-emotional skills, intrinsic motivation, and the love of learning needed to be economically successful.

Chapter 9

Leading to Innovation

I'd like a taco. I will pick up my phone and order a taco, and a taco-copter drone will deliver it to my home within ten minutes. Or maybe I need a part for my broken chair. I will take a picture of the broken part, review a menu of options for replacement, and produce the part I need on my home 3-D printer. Or maybe I need a ride to the airport. So I order an autonomous vehicle to give me a ride. All these ideas were ridiculous a few years ago, but are becoming amazingly possible because of the rate of development of ideas and technologies.

We are in the age of innovation, except in schools, where we persist in arguing about which set of one-size-fits-all content coverage standards to require for all kids of a given age. Will all of these examples become reality before we achieve the change to high-quality, personalized competency-based learning systems?

> **The reasonable man adapts to the world; the unreasonable one persists in trying to adapt the world to himself. Therefore, all progress depends on the unreasonable man.**
>
> **—George Bernard Shaw**

Let's be unreasonable, and consider the many ways in which education leaders could become un-stuck, and begin to encourage innovation in our schools.

FOCUS ON THE LEARNER

Since the beginning of American public education, we have focused on what to cover for each age group. Competency-based learning depends on a different focus. By knowing the learning needs of each student, schools can work with parents to create plans for learning that maximize the student's growth and progress, tap into student interests, and fully prepare students for higher levels of learning. Using explicit competency progressions allows us to track the learning progress of individual students and offer instruction at their level of readiness for as long as needed.

As schools develop explicit pathways to higher-level skills and clear criteria for competency at each step along the pathway, students can have well-defined learning goals. This is the first step toward maximizing student learning, according to Marzano, Schmoker, Hattie, DuFour, and many other authors.

USE DATA THAT MATTERS

Since the school reform era began in the 1980s, we have used data to rank students and compare schools, districts, states, and subgroups. Standardized assessment produces percentile scores that are designed to compare and rank. Some of this data is important, but we have yet to make it valuable by changing our adult behaviors in response to student data in a way that significantly improves student outcomes.

By far the most important information to improve learning outcomes is formative data. Assessment is formative only if the data is used to help educators design and redesign instruction on a frequent basis, which means at least weekly or daily. Learning to systematically collect formative data and then apply it to the ongoing design of instruction is one of the essential tools for competency-based learning.

AIM HIGHER

If you are the Detroit public schools, and only 5 percent of fourth graders are proficient in reading, and 4 percent are proficient in math, and statistically 0 percent of students are in the advanced range for either reading or math, small incremental improvements are not enough. **It is time to stop tweaking the one-size-fits-all debacle**.

We are a nation in which only about one-third of students are proficient readers in the fourth grade, in which only one-fifth of poor students are proficient readers in the fourth grade, in which 7 percent of African American twelfth graders are proficient in math, in which 75 percent of high school graduates are ineligible for military service, in which millions of jobs go unfilled because of a mismatch between skill requirements and the available workforce.

Aim high or go home. Help 80 percent of our students become solid grade-level readers and mathematicians. Help every child develop a love of reading and learning. Help children develop intrinsic motivation, the capacity for self-regulation, strong bodies, and calm minds. Build a system that will allow every child to grow and learn at the optimal rate for that individual.

Create a nation of learners, men and women of character, who can deal with the complexities of the age of information, technology, and innovation.

HIRE AND KEEP GREAT PEOPLE

Many factors influence a student's academic performance, including individual experiences and family and community characteristics. But research clearly suggests that, among school-related factors, teachers matter most. When it comes to student performance on reading and math tests, a teacher is estimated to have two to three times the impact of any other school factor, including services, facilities, and even school leadership.

High-quality teachers are the hallmark of successful education systems. And yet recent iterations of American education reform have focused on providing negative consequences for struggling schools rather than providing incentives and recognition for success. Teacher satisfaction rates are low. Many teachers and administrators have reported leaving the profession because there is just not much joy anymore, and because the culture of schools has become negative, fear-driven, and anxious. Many bright young men and women reject the possibility of becoming a teacher because of the lack of appreciation and respect for teachers and the poor pay in compared to other professions.

Innovative leaders can find ways to hire and keep great people if they develop systems in which educators:

- Are treated as valuable professionals
- Work in a culture of trust, collaboration, and innovation
- Have time to continue learning and developing professional skills
- Earn reasonable pay compared to other professions

But innovative leaders at the district level will not be able to impact the overall national climate for attracting the best and brightest to our profession.

State and national policy leaders can learn from some of the best international systems that offer educators the prestige and professionalism, which help attract top quality candidates.

Finland has very high standards to enter teacher preparation programs, and admits only about 10 percent of the students who apply. Teacher salaries in Finland are fairly average for EU countries, but teachers have the satisfaction of being admitted to a high-status profession, working with thoughtful and innovative colleagues, and having the professional autonomy to respond to the learning needs of their students. Finland has a very high retention rate for teachers, with about 90 percent of trained teachers remaining in the profession for the duration of their careers.

Singapore selects prospective teachers from the top one-third of their secondary school class. Trainees receive a stipend equivalent to 60 percent of a teacher's salary while in training and commit to teaching for a minimum of three years. Singapore also actively recruits mid-career candidates. The Ministry of Education supports ongoing professional development, and more than 30 percent of Singapore's teachers get performance-based bonuses.

England had struggled to attract high-quality candidates into teacher training and developed a multilevel strategy, including awards programs on television, alternate certification models to compete with traditional university teacher training programs, and bonuses to teach in high-need communities. As a result, teaching went from the ninety-second career choice to the top career choice within five years (Barber & Mourshed, 2007).

Given the evidence that great teachers have profound effects on the lifetime outcomes of their students, it is important that we find ways to attract and keep the best possible candidates for teaching. **This will never happen by clinging to the negative culture of our high-pressure one-size-fits-all instruction by coverage model**. Change to a dynamic competency-based learning model depends on our ability to bring thinkers and innovators back into our profession.

BUILD A CULTURE OF LEARNING

The Taylorian top-down model depended on management authority to enforce the **one best way** of industrial production. Schools adopted those same management structures, and in recent years departments of education have used requirements for research-based and evidence-based practices to reinforce state and federal edicts by requiring top-down approvals. Classroom teachers have been given the clearest message: Follow the script, cover the units, stick with the program, do what you are told.

But national data clearly shows an absence of any significant improvement in education outcomes since the early 1970s. Rigid top-down authoritarian school reform has resulted in no improvement at all. Our schools are the quintessential holdouts in a world of learning and change.

As we transition to personalized competency-based learning systems, we must find a way to break this pattern and begin to listen to our teachers, our parents, and our students. In many schools this means building a new culture from scratch.

The adults in a school must be an exemplary model of excitement for learning, intrinsic motivation, collaboration, positive communication, innovation, using technology to invent new ways to learn, personalized learning, and using data to drive change. **A culture of innovation depends on building a culture in which we feel safe and connected, able to speak up, share ideas, make mistakes, and learn together**. We should model what we want students to become so that they can be successful in a world of ongoing learning and change.

Invest in training for your staff. Start with clear learning goals, clear expectations for the essential knowledge and skills you want each member of your staff to have. Beyond minimum essential knowledge and skill, allow each individual to choose areas of expertise they personally wish to develop so that they can serve as mentors and leaders within your organization. Train your people in how to generate, how to evaluate, and how to implement innovative ideas so that your organization continues to grow and improve.

RECOGNIZE RISK-TAKERS

The do what-you-are-told culture that has developed in many schools is antithetical to a culture that values risk-takers. But according to Mark Zuckerberg, Elon Musk, Jeff Bezos, and many others in the modern tech era, those who do not take chances are on the path to "guaranteed failure." Change is a necessary part of progress. Without growth our systems become rigid, inflexible, and predictable.

We can certainly predict what our schools will be like if we continue to cling to the old CTS model. More of the same, and those predictable outcomes are crushing the futures of our children and stifling the development of our economy.

Some say that our predictable school environments have attracted risk-averse teachers. Perhaps, but scratch the surface and in every school you will likely find men and women with the capacity for mindful risk.

Risk-takers

- **Don't accept the status quo**
- **Are in touch with a greater purpose in life**
- **Are curious**
- **Focus on adding value**
- **Value other people's talents and like to collaborate with them**
- **Demonstrate grit and perseverance**
- **Exhibit a growth mind-set**
- **Believe great things are possible**
- **Can shake off mistakes and embrace the learning opportunity**

As we transition toward competency-based learning systems, education leaders will need to find, keep, and nurture the risk-takers who will help us take on the challenge of a lifetime. Praise and recognize them. Send a message that challenging the way things are done is welcomed.

REWARD FAILURE

Nothing crushes originality like a fear of failure. But innovation requires that we try things without absolutely knowing how they will turn out, and that a near-miss, a partial failure, or a major flop allows you to learn so that your next attempt will be better informed.

Fear of failure in the education business has caused many districts/ states to pretend (lie, fabricate, misinform) that every program we try has been a success. With pretense there is no acknowledgment of the mistakes we could correct, no institutional learning, no progress, and no positive change. Share everything, all the successes and all the failures so you can learn from them.

Staff is rewarded for trying new ideas at Google X, the secret innovation laboratory that takes on "moonshot" projects. Proctor and Gamble has its "heroic failure" award. TATA has a "dare to try" award. In a school that innovates, leaders will embrace those who are willing to try, willing to look honestly at the data, willing to learn, and willing to try again.

SET GOALS FOR INNOVATION

An organization that values innovation will use metrics for innovation and include them in its annual scorecard. These might include number of ideas generated, number of prototypes in trial, new products or practices, and the intervening time between idea evaluation and implementation. People do what gets measured; so measure innovation.

When developing ideas for innovation, consider this five-step process:

1. Understand and clearly define what your students need. These could be skill levels, exposure to ideas, experiences, behavioral habits, and habits of mind.
2. Contrast the desired outcome with what your school is consistently achieving today.
3. Identify gaps in the outcomes and experiences you aspire to achieve and what you typically achieve.
4. Wisely pick a small number of factors for which innovation is needed.
5. Create specific goals that align to the factors you wish to improve. Make them clear, measurable, and achievable within a reasonable time.

BORROW WITH PRIDE

Learn from others. We are in this era of innovation because of our ability to exchange ideas quickly and easily. What in past centuries took decades for research, theories, and new ideas to be shared can now be shared in months, weeks, or days.

Build networks with like-minded innovators. Avoid the pretense that you already know and are doing everything anyone could possibly do for your students.

Observe other teachers, schools, districts, and organizations and copy their best practice. Find the best minds in education innovation and contact them regularly. Have a deliberate policy for sourcing innovations from outside your own schools and proudly share the story of innovation within your organization. Look for ideas everywhere!

HAVE A MISSION THAT MATTERS

In 1922 Dr. Laura Cushman opened a school on the porch of her home on Biscayne Boulevard in Miami. Her philosophy guided her as the school grew.

Our first aim is that all teachers and pupils in our school should preserve a happy attitude. We believe that a child whose environment is conducive to character development and intellectual growth

is a happy child. If a child is not happy, we will seek the underlying causes without ceasing until he or she is adjusted satisfactorily.

A school seeks to develop the child mentally, physically, and in character growth. To do this, the child must be placed in happy surroundings, be properly adjusted to his work, and have wholesome participation in living experiences. The creation of such a school life is our aim.

With a clear vision of the school she wanted, she set the following standards for staff and student behavior.

- **A happy attitude**
- **Acceptance of the tasks of growing and learning as a personal responsibility**
- **Industry and perseverance in accomplishing these accepted tasks**
- **Honesty with self and with others in every phase of living**
- **Growth in ability to attack learning problems and to use judgment in changing situations**
- **Self-control and poise**
- **Wholesome personal habits**
- **An attitude that seeks to understand others' points of view and is ever tolerant and kind**
- **Gracious, unfailing courtesy**
- **Appreciations that enrich life**

A century later, Laura Cushman's school continues to thrive. Her mission was clear. She found staff who understood and supported this mission, and have continued it to this day. The culture in this school is conducive to trust, safety, connection, collaboration, problem-solving, intrinsic motivation, positivity, and lifelong learning.

The most extraordinary people in the world today don't have a career. They have a mission.

—Vishen Lakhiani

Disciplined innovation is an essential ingredient of a successful competency-based learning system. With clear outcomes in mind, and with a careful awareness of the needs of each student, the competency-based teacher develops a teaching/learning plan, implements, and then uses formative assessment to discover that it worked better for some students than for others. Some students need more time, and the disciplined innovator figures a way to give them more time. Some students develop proficiency in a skill far more quickly than expected, and the disciplined innovator moves those students forward to more challenging skills and content. Some students don't respond well at all to the instructional plan. It's a miss. Rather than blame those students, the disciplined teacher-innovator considers others ways to teach every crucial concept or skill.

Whatever it takes! Any amount of time, in or out of school, in groups or on a screen, using paper or using manipulatives, the disciplined innovator finds a way to help students learn.

> **Imagine if we allowed the talented men and women who are professional educators to become disciplined innovators, work in a culture of respect, take risks, know their students, and make a professional assessment of each student's learning needs. Imagine if we attracted the best and brightest of our young adults to a profession that was a model of innovation and collaboration, allowing them to build pathways to student success and social justice.**

We are living at a moment in time when great change is possible. Schools have the potential to be the instrument by which children become lifelong learners, strong men and women of character, problem-solvers, empathetic listeners, and leaders in the world. Schools have the potential to give opportunity to those poor or vulnerable students who are being failed today in such great numbers. But positive change will occur only if we seize this moment of opportunity, believe we can be the change, and then make it happen.

Chapter 10

The Equity Agenda

Let's devise a plan that will systematically damage the learning future of poor and minority students, while making it look like the fault is entirely theirs.

1. Use a one-size-fits-all curriculum approach, so that we can pretend everyone is getting the same learning opportunity even while we know that many kids are not developmentally prepared to be successful at that level of instruction. Use lines like, "All students have a right to rigorous high-quality content standards," to shut up those who might question our approach.
2. Make the curriculum and pacing guide so aggressive that there is no opportunity for teachers to give serious attention to understanding or remediating an individual student's learning delays. Suggest that "high-quality teachers can cover more content than low-quality teachers" to obfuscate the reality that racing through content makes no sense at all.
3. Use scripted instructional programs, rigid pacing guides, district assessment schedules, and mandatory annual standardized testing to put the pressure on teachers to keep up with the standardized delivery of a standardized content system. Without telling them, take professional discretion and problem-solving out of the teaching profession. Make them behave like automatons.
4. Using the same approach, make sure kids know that school is about learning what we tell them to learn. Turn students into passive recipients of what we deem to be worth learning.
5. Keep students in age-based grades so that we can consistently sort them into winners and losers. First we cover, then we test, then we sort. And repeat. Give vulnerable students the message that they are among the learning "losers" many thousands of times.

6. Sometimes a great teacher can make a connection with a student that causes him or her to give incredible effort to being successful in school. Diminish the likelihood of this happening by making the pace of instruction so fast so that teachers do not have time to build relationships, teach prosocial classroom behaviors, establish positive classroom routines, and help the students bond as a team to support each other.

7. Each year, as vulnerable students fall further behind, require that all students move to the same higher levels of instructional challenge. Even in a school with a large majority of students who are several years behind in their reading or math skills, move to more challenging content in which they are likely to be frustrated.

8. As students get frustrated, they are more likely to disengage from learning and misbehave. Create an angry, frustrated, punitive adult environment in the school so that school staff is more likely to respond with anger to misbehavior rather than trying to understand why the student is choosing to misbehave.

9. Marginalize parents. Keep giving them the message that we know what their kids need. Avoid asking for their input regarding their children's academic, social, and behavior needs.

10. Use bureaucratic requirements to overwhelm school leaders who might want to innovate, create more humane teaching and learning environments, or respond to the individual learning needs of students.

11. Construct a funding system that manages to offer fewer resources to students who need the most instructional support.

12. Use economic and safety incentives to keep the best teachers in the most affluent communities.

Somewhere in Flint a committee is meeting to consider replacing the standardized middle school math program that has been failing them for years. Student scores on the M-STEP exam have been lousy. Teachers complain that there is too much content to cover in the time allowed, and that they were never properly trained to use the program.

After months of meeting, the committee chooses between two different standardized middle school math programs. Both claim to be "evidence-based." Both are correlated to the sixth-, seventh-, and eighth-grade CCSS math standards, proving that they cover all the standards.

In fact, both of them are terrific and thoughtful programs for kids who have the prerequisite math skills. But a majority of kids in the district are not at that readiness level, lack fundamental number sense or basic math concepts, and are unlikely to understand the lessons. With urging and cajoling from their teachers, some students could learn to memorize the protocol (a series of steps) to solve some of the math problems in each of the competing math

programs, but in most cases they would find an answer without really understanding the process they have followed.

A winner is chosen. It happens to be an updated version of the math program they used almost fifteen years ago, but which was discontinued because
of poor outcomes. All things come around. Because of budget problems,
the district can afford to buy the math program but cannot fund full training
of the middle school math teachers. The materials are delivered before any
teacher training has begun. Teachers are given this year's pacing guide and
NWEA assessment schedule before they have had any time to examine the
new math program. Teachers are upset and angry. Math coaches are expected
to help teachers learn to use the new program on the fly as the new school
year begins.

Somewhere in Tampa a committee is meeting to consider a recent update
to the Mathematics Florida Standards (MAFS) and the Language Arts Florida
Standards (LAFS). The committee is responsible for effectively implementing the newest iteration of the content standards that must be used in each
grade and course. In response to the changes there will be updates to some of
the course syllabi, and pacing guides must be adjusted to ensure that every
standard is properly covered.

In grade 7, as an example, teachers are expected to **teach/cover** enormous
amounts of content. Delivering all these content standards is done in the name
of rigor:

- Dance/60 standards
- English language arts/102 standards
- English language development/5 standards
- Gifted/284 standards
- Health education/36 standards
- Mathematics/32 standards
- Music/47 standards
- Physical education/37 standards
- Science/107 standards
- Social studies/67 standards
- Special skills/265 standards
- Theater/66 standards
- Visual art/58 standards
- World languages/378 standards

Beginning with these incredible lists of content standards, the district will
develop its version of the **one best way**. Learning programs and materials
will be chosen. Curriculum maps, pacing guides, and assessment schedules
will be developed. The state will maintain pressure on the districts through

its use of annual standardized assessment, teacher evaluation requirements, and school rating systems.

A few of the hundreds of Florida grade 7 content standards are listed next. Read the list. See if you understand the standard, how to teach it, and what a successful learning outcome would look like. Are most seventh graders ready for and interested in the content of these standards?

MAFS.7.EE.1.1/Apply properties of operations as strategies to add, subtract, factor, and expand linear expressions with rational coefficients.

HE.7.C.1.2/Explain how physical, mental/emotional, social, and intellectual dimensions of health are interrelated.

LAFS.68.RST.2.4/Determine the meaning of symbols, key terms, and other domain-specific words and phrases as they are used in a specific scientific or technical context relevant to grades 6–8 texts and topics.

SC.68.CS-CP.1.1/Define parameters for individual and collaborative projects using Boolean logic (e.g., using "not," "or," "and").

SS.7.C.1.1/Recognize how Enlightenment ideas including Montesquieu's view of separation of power and John Locke's theories related to natural law and how Locke's social contract influenced the founding fathers.

VA.68.C.3.2/Examine and compare the qualities of artworks and utilitarian objects to determine their aesthetic significance.

Florida, like most states, defines what **must be covered** for all seventh graders. When the state updates/changes the coverage standards, districts must adjust teaching materials, syllabi, lesson plans, and pacing guides to ensure that it all gets "covered." **And it will be covered**. Somehow teachers will claw their way through these hundreds of grade-level content standards, often with students who are so far behind and so disengaged.

There are no standards for learning in the Florida state advisory material, which would be a precise understanding of what needs to be learned and how deep understanding or application of knowledge/skills could be demonstrated. Instead teachers will once again double down on the imperative of "coverage" for the standards they have been given. Teachers will not be advised to determine what their students know and are ready to learn because the state has given them clear directions about what to cover regardless of student readiness. Ready or not, here comes the standard curriculum.

In districts across the nation there are committees working diligently to ensure that some version of the *one best way* of instruction for all students is fully implemented. "If you don't cover it, they can't learn it" is the unquestioned foundation for these efforts. We continue to put incredible effort into maintaining a system that is only marginally effective for our most fortunate students and is causing incredible harm to our most vulnerable.

By now the research is abundantly clear:

- **The many versions of exhaustive sets of one-size-fits-all content coverage standards have not produced significantly improved learning outcomes for all students or vulnerable students.**
- **Aggressive annual standardized testing of students has not produced significantly improved learning outcomes for all students or vulnerable students.**
- **Aggressive annual evaluation of teachers has not produced significantly improved learning outcomes for all students or vulnerable students.**
- **Adjusting pacing guides, updating curriculum alignment, writing CCSS goals on the whiteboard, pressuring teachers to teach faster, reducing or eliminating art, music, recess, physical education, and time for social-emotional learning have not produced significantly improved outcomes for all students or vulnerable students.**
- **Compliance with federal school reform initiatives to date has not improved learning outcomes for all American students or vulnerable students.**

What we are doing to poor and other vulnerable children across the nation is just plain wrong. The impact of using our one-size-fits-all instructional model on poor kids is well demonstrated. Poor kids, or kids with any handicap or delay in development, are getting crushed in our standardized system of education.

Just over half of public school children are eligible for free/reduced price lunches. These children come from families with incomes at or below 130 percent of the poverty level. That is a lot of students who are predictably more likely to come to school with less-developed language, sensory-motor, and self-regulation skills.

Poverty is just one of the significant factors that are associated with vulnerability to school failure. Many students with the potential to be good learners fall behind the rigid pace of instruction, begin to get frustrated, and then disengage from learning. **In our existing coverage-driven system, a significant majority of students are failing to develop the knowledge and skills that are a necessary foundation for success in the age of learning, information, and technology.**

Competency-based models use an approach that is fundamentally different from the traditional structure of the American school system. Rather than requiring all learners to be exposed to the same overwhelming content standards in the same grade, students progress at different rates and only by demonstrating mastery of important learning objectives or competencies. Students get all the time, instruction, support needed to achieve a deep understanding of essential content or skills. Students can learn and improve skills at school, at home, or in other parts of the community. All students are held to the same high expectations for learning crucial content, but instruction is individualized to meet each person's strengths and challenges.

Equity is a fundamental goal of competency-based education. This design allows students with diverse backgrounds and learning experiences to reach essential academic and other learning goals at any pace necessary. Competency-based learning allows students all the time and opportunity needed to reach each goal along the pathway to higher outcomes. Some learners advance more quickly than others. Other students continue to work on each topic or skill until they demonstrate mastery.

In most CTS public schools today, students are never required to demonstrate competency in essential skills that lead to higher-level skills. Instead, units are covered, tests are given, grades are assigned, and then the class moves on. As a result, many students fall farther behind each year.

While competency-based learning systems are still in their infancy, there are clear reasons why they have the capacity to create a **better opportunity for vulnerable students** to become successful learners.

1. We will always have students with differences in knowledge and skill. Competency-based learning takes students where they are, identifies learning needs and readiness levels, offers instruction matched to the needs of each student, carefully monitors progress, and moves on to higher levels of learning as soon as a student is fully ready. Vulnerable students are not left behind.
2. Establishing clear learning goals is motivating. When a student has a clear understanding of the next learning goal and understands that with practice and effort he or she will be able to become fully competent, motivation is increased. Success leads to success.
3. A competency-based learning system allows for teachers to respond to the needs of students quickly. Students don't have to fail for a semester or a year before having another chance to deeply learn important content. Many competency-based schools build in flex hours or instructional match time during the day to make sure that students get the timely support they need.
4. Competency education is a comprehensive approach that serves the needs of vulnerable students, typical students, and gifted students. Indeed,

programs for gifted students have often incorporated the elements of competency-based learning. Special needs students are also well served in a competency-based learning model. The Early Learning Success Initiative (Sornson, 2007; Sornson, Frost, & Burns, 2005) demonstrated that using an early competency model with students at-risk of failure in the early grades resulted in much reduced need to refer and place students into special education, with a resulting cost savings of millions annually to the district.

5. Competency education embraces the growth mind-set that is necessary for eradicating inequity. Students are not labeled as learning winners or losers in the early years. Kids develop at different rates and in different ways. Competency embraces these differences and allows for each child to progress at the rate that allows them to continue to be a successful learner.

Competency education is not going to have all the answers, and it is certainly going to have its own unintended consequences. Some observers fear that higher-income students will benefit from competency-based learning, allowing them to take advantage of their access to books, learning time with parents, technology, digital learning systems, private instruction, workshops and camps. Indeed, these students will have much improved opportunities to advance to higher levels of learning.

But competency-based learning, with its emphasis on student ownership and respect for different rates of development, will allow less advantaged students to maintain the growth mind-set, avoid getting locked into a belief that they are poor learners, and have the opportunity to reach any high-level learning skill they wish to pursue.

> **It is especially important to use CBL systems in the PK to grade 3 early childhood learning years. These are the years in which the trajectory of learning for life is established, where habits of mind and beliefs about yourself as a learner are established. Just a few years of frustration and failure is enough to damage vulnerable young children in a way that no competency-based secondary school learning system could heal.**

Looking to the future, in the age of information, learning, and technology, fortunate students who have good learning skills, good work skills, and love to learn will have incredible opportunities to find good jobs and economic success. But our present CTS system is not built to help all kids love to learn.

The CTS system is willing to feed vulnerable students breakfast and lunch, but is not willing to give them the instruction they need at their level, so that they have a chance to become successful learners. The majority of children who struggle and fail to thrive in our present educational system will not be ready for the learning future, and will be relegated to low-skill, low-wage lifetimes. By focusing on the development of essential learning outcomes and building clear pathways to higher-level skills, competency-based learning systems have the potential to give all our kids a chance to become successful learners for life.

For how many more decades will we crush the opportunity for poor and vulnerable children to learn and prosper?

Chapter 11

Bring Back the Joy

The vocabulary of school reform includes *standards, assessment, results, research-based, focused instruction, accountability,* and *data*. It soon becomes abundantly clear that school reformers are focused on actions that may link to improved scores on a school, district, state, or national standardized assessment summary. *Get better test scores* is the underlying imperative. The message has been clearly communicated to schools across the nation, and the pressure is palpable.

Curriculum directors, principals, teachers, and even students feel the pressure to get better scores. Tweak the pacing guide, adopt a new math program, or swear allegiance to a different set of grade-level content coverage expectations. Evaluate the teachers more aggressively, threaten to fire the principal, or add more test prep to the curriculum.

> **What if there was a missing piece, something we all know in our bones to be crucial for high-level learning, crucial for students to have ownership over their own learning, crucial for students to enjoy learning and to fall in love with learning for life?**

One of the things that set children apart from many adults is their enormous capacity for joy. A three-year-old playing in the waves at the beach. An eight-year-old climbing a tree, or on a swing, or playing catch. A five-year-old listening to a story. The ability to become deeply absorbed and to derive pleasure from that level of engagement is something most adults wish they could recapture.

As Steven Wolk (2008) asked, if the experience of "doing school" destroys children's spirit to learn, their sense of wonder, their curiosity about the world, and their willingness to care for the human condition, have we succeeded as educators, no matter how well our students do on standardized tests?

The irony is that joyful learning is often viewed as time away from the more "serious" work of education. But really, joyful learning is a necessary partner in any school design that leads to student agency and self-efficacy, to higher rates of learning, and to developing the skills and habits of mind of a lifelong learner. None of this is news.

Joyful learning is a fundamental part of Montessori, Waldorf, and Reggio-Emilia learning systems. It was observed by Piaget, Erickson, and Vygotsky as an essential part of the childhood experience of learning through play. Early childhood educators have long noted an important truth: children who fall in love with learning are more motivated, engaged, independent, and successful learners throughout their lives. Most young children are naturally hungry to learn. The desire to know and to understand is considered a basic need (Maslow, 1954; Hawking, 1988).

> **The success of competency-based learning will in large part be associated with how well we take the race out of teaching and learning, consider the needs of the whole child, and build learning systems that cultivate the experiences of learning and teaching with joy. Better test scores will be a paltry by-product of much more respectful and effective learning environments.**

A child's emotional state has a powerful effect on learning. High states of anxiety or fear are associated with raised levels of cortisol and norepinephrine. The fight or flight response state diminishes a child's ability to sustain attention, decrease short-term and long-term memory, reduce listening skills, and problem-solving skills. Persistent high levels of fear and anxiety have a negative effect on health and well-being, and disrupt the developing architecture of the brain during the early learning years. Optimal capacity for learning is possible only in an environment in which students feel safe and connected.

Thoughtful teachers:

- take the time to get to know their students
- allow students to get to know them
- build a predictable and secure classroom culture
- develop classroom routines that help every student learn the behaviors that lead to success

* practice these routines until they are consistently used by every student
* and create opportunities for students to build relationships with each other

With a positive classroom culture in place students are more likely to:

* feel safe and secure that in this place no one will hurt or embarrass them
* stay engaged
* be respectful of others
* respect classroom routines
* take ownership and make efforts to learn

Mihaly Csikszentmihalyi (1996) wrote about the value of *flow*, a state of being associated with energized focus, full involvement, intrinsic motivation, and success in the process of the activity. Great educators can cultivate these moments by ensuring safety, planning instruction that responds to the readiness of our students, offering choice when possible, and by building on a child's interests and passions. Great teachers know that we will see more of these moments if we protect learning time in which students collaborate, learn to talk and socialize with each other, discover connections to nature, enjoy movement, and make choices. Every moment of flow in the classroom experiences of a young student improves the odds that he or she will fall in love with learning.

Dr. Barbara Fredrickson's (1998, 2001, 2003, 2009) *Broaden-and-Build Theory* explains how increasing positive emotions creates an upward spiral that leads not only to future positive emotions but also to more open, creative, and flexible thinking processes, enhanced psychological strengths (like being more resilient, accepting, and more driven by purpose), better social connections, and even better physical health.

Fredrickson and Losada (2005) describe the ratio of positive to negative emotions needed to get the *Broaden and Build* effect. In the workplace, individuals with flourishing mental health and higher performance were found to experience 2.9 or more positive emotions for every one negative emotional experience. The application of this understanding to the learning environment is obvious. High-performance learning is more likely if you have a high ratio of positive emotional experiences in the classroom, characterized by success and joy.

Competency-based learning gives us an opportunity to put joy back into the classroom. By eliminating the requirement to cover long lists of academic content expectations, with the knowledge that students are steadily moving from one clear learning objective to the next along a pathway to higher-level skills, the race through chapters and units is over. Because of the far greater efficacy of the competency model, there is plenty of time available to help develop the whole child and bring joy to every learning day.

Joy usually requires some ownership on the part of the learner. It is generally unhurried, and often involves movement and play. Time for nature, freedom to choose, discovery, beauty, social learning, social play, collaboration, invention, tinkering, creation of beauty, building things that work, and finding out what does not work can become part of our school culture at all levels of learning.

Reverence for children is reverence for life.

—Shinichi Suzuki

A new model is emerging. It is designed with an understanding of the importance of allowing children to experience high rates of learning success. It is built to help students achieve a deep understanding of clear and crucial learning goals. It is informed by a solid understanding of a child's readiness for learning, and by the commitment to give students what they need at their instructional level for as long as it takes. Its architecture includes pathways to competency, sometimes different for one student than another. In this model, learning is for life, and must be based on the joyful engagement of the learner.

We wish to help our children become learners for life. As Sir Ken Robinson (2013) has superbly stated, "The answer is not to standardize education, but to personalize and customize it to the needs of each child and community. There is no alternative. There never was."

Chapter 12

We Need Leaders Like You

WE NEED YOU

We need the best and brightest, the shining stars, those women and men with the capacity to reinvent our schools and build a competency model in which teachers love to teach and students love to learn.

Great teachers always make a difference. Even when using a one-size-fits-all coverage-driven model, great teachers inspire better learning. But for a competency model to work, we need educators who know their students, support different ways to learn, differentiate instruction, coach students, prepare individual learning plans, offer choices, carefully monitor progress, support student learning until a deep understanding of essential learning objectives is achieved, advance students as soon as they are ready, work with parents to build learning teams, collaborate with other educators, build more positive school and classroom cultures, and model lifetime learning.

This is not some minor reform; it's a revolution in practice. We need dynamic change agents to build competency pathways to higher-level skills that matter, design instructional systems that allow students to make personal choices that impact their own learning, maximize the potential of each student, and turn kids onto learning for life.

> **Great vision without great people is irrelevant.**
>
> **—Jim Collins, author of *Good to Great***

We've dumbed down, de-professionalized, and demeaned educators with our emphasis on one-size-fits-all one-best-way scripted and rigidly paced

Figure 12.1.   We Need You, Pixabay, KraeheMicha, CC0

instructional systems. In a competency-based learning system we will need teachers who do much more than passively be told what to teach, how to teach it, how to assess, and when to assess. A competency-based learning system will be built with solid professional educators who love to figure out the complexities of helping every child learn essential skills and helping all children find a pathway to higher-level skills that allows them to build a great life for themselves.

Our goal is not to tweak a few extra points on the school average state assessment score. **Our goal is to build a system based on a personalized competency-based design that allows every student to optimize his or her academic, behavioral, and social-emotional learning outcomes.**

To attract this corps of confident, collaborative, innovative education professionals we are going to have to turn some things around.

Teacher Quality and Teacher Shortage

High-performing national systems like those of Finland, Singapore, and South Korea recruit all (100%) of their teachers from the top third of their academic cohort. This extraordinary selectivity is just part of the integrated approach to attracting, training, and keeping quality educators, which adds to the prestige of the teaching profession in these nations.

Lack of prestige is just one of the reasons many bright stars in the United States are not interested in becoming professional educators. Low salaries, organizational culture, and lack of teacher control over what and how to teach help keep many potential leaders from becoming teachers.

In recent years the number of overall teacher preparation students is in decline. In my home state, Michigan State University saw its teacher-prep enrollment fall 45 percent between 2010 and 2014, from 1,659 to 911. Grand Valley State University's enrollment tumbled by 67 percent, from 751 to 248 in the same period (Derringer, 2017). From 2008 to 2018, the total number of Michigan college students studying to become a teacher declined by more than 50 percent.

The state of California experienced a 53 percent reduction in teacher prep enrollments between 2008–2009 and 2012–2013. The number of students who say they will major in education has reached its lowest point in forty-five years, according to data gathered by the UCLA's Cooperative Institutional Research Program (Eagan et al., 2016). Just 4.2 percent intend to major in education—a typical first step to becoming a teacher—compared to 11 percent in 2000; 10 percent in 1990; and 11 percent in 1971.

Keeping teachers has also become a challenge. Our profession has become "a leaky bucket," according to the Learning Policy Institute (Sutcher, Darling-Hammond, & Carver-Thomas, 2016), losing about 8 percent of our teacher workforce every academic year. According to Ingersoll (2001, 2002), those who report leaving because of job dissatisfaction cite low salaries, lack of support from school administration, lack of student motivation, student discipline problems, and lack of teacher influence over decision making as factors influencing their decisions.

After relatively flat national student enrollment figures for more than a decade, the National Center for Education Statistics (NCES) predicts the school-going population will increase by roughly three million students in the next decade. We need great teachers at a time when fewer students are going into education and when the profession has become a leaky bucket.

Building a System That Can Attract and Keep the Shining Stars We Need in Our Schools

Attracting shining stars to a system that is broken and that clings to an antiquated model of learning that most students can't wait to escape is not the focus of this chapter. Our focus, instead, is on **finding shining stars to build a new system** based on personalized competency-based learning.

Job description: Innovative, collaborative, dynamic change agents are wanted to build a new model for teaching and learning in the age of information and technology.

Main Job Tasks and Responsibilities

- understand the learning needs of each student
- understand the skills and steps needed to develop in each domain of student learning
- plan, prepare, and deliver instructional activities that match student needs at the instructional level that will optimize learning
- monitor student learning regularly
- maintain data that accurately describes student learning progress and readiness
- adjust instruction based on progress
- allow students the time needed to develop deep understanding and application of crucial skills and content
- move students forward as soon as they are ready for more challenging material
- support growth mind-set and self-efficacy among students
- develop positive class and school culture
- build strong positive relationships with students
- establish clear positive classroom procedures and routines
- develop the whole child, including social-emotional, behavioral, and self-regulation skills associated with school and life success
- collaborate to develop clear learning objectives on a pathway to higher-level skills
- identify and select different instructional resources and methods to meet students' varying needs
- use relevant technology to support instruction
- work with parents to determine student strengths and learning needs, and to support home learning
- collaborate with staff to build ongoing professional learning systems
- establish personal learning plans leading to competency at higher-level professional skills

Key Competencies

- love to learn
- verbal and written communication skills
- tech skills

- **problem-solving skills**
- **collaboration**
- **ongoing observational assessment**
- **using data to drive instruction**
- **building individual competency-based learning plans with students**
- **social-emotional intelligence**
- **capacity for managing change and innovation**

Ready to Begin

- **as soon as possible**

Respect, prestige, and professionalism won't come to education by accident. We will build a professional culture for our schools only if we abandon a top-down, one-size-fits-all system that demeans both teachers and students. As we redesign our learning systems, we have an opportunity and responsibility to build a professional culture that aligns with the tenets of personalized competency-based learning.

1. **Hire bright and shining stars**. This might mean finding ways to attract the top third of graduating classes by improving starting pay, offering residency incentives, offering tax incentives or scholarships for teacher education at the bachelor's and master's levels, and waiving off student debt after a set of years in teaching. But it might also mean attracting bright and shining stars who are not high GPA students, but who exhibit the skills of technology, innovation, and entrepreneurship we want in our competency-based schools.
2. **Offer new teacher induction that matters**. Year-long residencies, long-term intensive coaching with master teachers, and significant on-site training might help build new teacher capacity to be a real success in the early part of a career.
3. **Establish clear competency-based criteria for hiring**, for earning tenure, and for becoming teacher-leaders. As of now, only a few districts have established basic competency criteria for hiring. Most have continued to rely on a credentialing system that puts great emphasis on passing courses, but does not have minimum standards for all essential entry-level skills. Districts might also develop competency standards for earning tenure or teacher-leader status, with corresponding increases in pay and responsibility.
4. **Offer professional development to meet the individual learning needs of each teacher**. Once competency standards are established,

teachers will have a clear set of learning goals they want to meet or exceed. Rather than random acts of professional development, professional learning could be aligned with the learning needs of staff, and learning could become an anytime anyplace event.

5. **Create professional support networks** to connect new teachers, and to connect teachers with similar interests. The power of social networks can help educators to support one another as they move from entry-level competency to higher-level skills.

6. **Put the "professional" back into our education profession**. Give teachers the responsibility to know their students and give them the instruction they need at their level. This is a foundation of the system in Finland and most other high-performing systems. Quit imposing top-down standardized instructional systems.

7. **Provide time for collaboration among faculty**. Once the assembly line model is vanquished and replaced by a model in which teachers and schools offer small group, blended, and project-based instruction as part of its menu of differentiated learning options, we can prioritize profession collaboration. The needs for professionals to refine pathways to competency at higher levels, to devise assessment and instructional options, and to share clear standards for competency make this a crucial step for competency-based schools.

8. **Build a safe, connected school culture**. Staff must feel safe and connected to become a high-performance team that is good at learning and problem - solving. Until staff experience a positive school culture, it is unlikely that students will be provided the positive culture needed for optimal learning.

9. **Reduce unnecessary bureaucracy and paperwork**. Cut the crap by at least 90 percent.

10. **Fire the bums**. Sadly there are a few educators who should not be around kids. We will never be a professional culture as long as we tolerate poor adult behavior. A positive school culture focuses on the positive much more than it spends time noticing the negative. But when there are substandard educator skills or behaviors we must protect the kids and protect the profession. Offer struggling educators a chance to improve, but if improvement is not forthcoming, invite them to find a different profession.

We need you, the shining stars, the innovators, the change-makers, the world-shakers, to overcome the obstacles to innovation and build a new model of purposeful and joyful learning for life. You may have been ready to flee the confines of a traditional school at one time in your life, but we need you to help change the basic design for learning and the culture of schools for adults and for students. **The time of greatest innovation, change, learning, collaborating, starting, fixing, improving, constantly improving our schools has begun.**

There could be no more exciting time to be an educator. If you love learning, if you are naturally good at teaching, if you want a challenge, if you want to create a better world for our children, become a part of the competency-based revolution.

Chapter 13

A Call to Action

In theory, the choice is simple. Continue to implement a time-bound, age-based, one-size-fits-all curriculum-driven instructional model that has not served us well for many decades. Or choose to develop a personalized competency-based learning system that identifies crucial learning outcomes, gives students the instruction and practice they need at their level of readiness, and monitors and adjusts instruction for as long as needed until competency is fully achieved.

For decades principals, teachers, and parents have had educational choices stripped away from them.

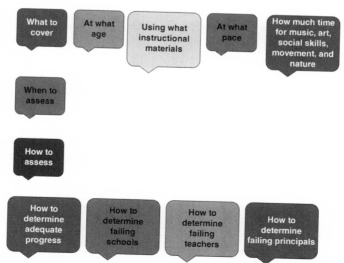

Figure 13.1.   Choices Taken Away from Educators

105

We have lived in the heyday of "the one best way" in our public schools as determined by politicians and bureaucrats. Educators have been stripped of both the authority and the responsibility to make professional decisions. Parents have been marginalized, and asked to passively accept inane content standards and assessment systems, along with joyless environments for learning. But the clear need for better learning outcomes has driven us to a unique moment of possibility.

Action is not worrying and whining.

It's leadership.
It's risk.
It's educating neighbors and colleagues.
It's planning. It's clarification.
It's learning to lead. It's taking over.
It's thoughtful deconstruction while rebuilding.
It's having a clear vision.
It's creating shared vision.
It's supporting others.
It's planning. It's mistakes. It's solving problems.
It's grit. It's long term.
Your goals will evolve.
It's overcoming resistance, ignorance, and apathy.
It comes from deep inside.

This book is a call to action, an advocacy for choices that better serve our children and our society. The time of greatest innovation, change, learning, collaborating, starting, fixing, improving, constantly improving our schools has begun.

But these are not always simple choices.

Can I stand up for competency within my school system which is built around an age-based coverage model that nobody seems to question?

Can I stand up for my child and demand a better learning system in a calm, thoughtful way that doesn't drive people away?

Should I close the classroom door and try to use some version of competency-based learning while also fulfilling the requirements of the district system and keeping my job?

Can I work with my child at home and do enough to mitigate the shortcomings of the school system?

Can I build classroom culture, slow down the race, and help students discover joyful learning while also fulfilling the requirements of the district system and keeping my job?

Can I help my child love learning so much at home that he or she is resilient to the boring or frustrating experiences he or she will find at school?

Should I advocate for change among my colleagues, principal, school board, parents, or community members?

How do I become a community leader and share a different vision for schools with my neighbors and friends?

Should I quit my dysfunctional system and start my own school?

Should I quit this dysfunctional system and find another school for my child?

Could I find a support network of like-minded educators and parents who can see the limitations of the system we have, and who want to build a different system, and are willing to do the work?

By responding to this call to action, educators, parents, and community leaders commit to building something that matters. Designing, building, improving, and sustaining competency-based learning systems is not a weekend event but rather a long-term process that must be guarded to maintain its integrity. Charlatans will attempt to correlate whatever they are selling with competency-based learning. Bureaucrats will try to snatch control from teachers, principals, students, and parents. Advocates for the CCSS (or any other set of content coverage standards) will pretend that their list of standards can be tweaked to become a competency framework.

It will take a clear shared vision to build our first generation of competency-based learning systems. Thoughtful leaders will build community, create a clear vision for what's possible, and then collaborate to bring their vision to life. (See appendix C.)

Not all competency-based learning systems will be alike. Just as neurodiversity allows students to learn in different ways, there will be diverse pathways that lead to the higher-level competencies we want for our children. This is a time for incredible innovation, creativity, and collaboration for educators and community leaders. Transformative ideas have lain dormant under a blanket of standardized one-best-way practices for more than a century and a half. No longer. Your understanding, commitment, and action will make it possible to build a new breed of learning systems with immensely positive outcomes for our communities and for our children.

The outcomes will include schools that are respectful and thoughtful places to work, learning systems that respect neurodiversity and protect vulnerable learners from harm. We have not yet begun to realize the potential of humans to learn. With personalized learning systems, so much more is possible. Leaders please step up; we need you now.

Chapter 14

Which System Do You Want for Your Children?

People and systems almost always resist change, and yet the change toward competency-based learning has clear momentum. Perhaps now we have reached a tipping point.

> **Choices are the hinges of destiny.**
>
> **—Edwin Markham**

For decades we have accepted the standardized one-best-way of curriculum-driven instruction. For most of us, it is the only system we know. But by reading from the beginning of this book to this chapter you now have an historical perspective, an awareness of the limits of curriculum-driven instruction, and a deeper understanding of the viability of competency-based learning. Here is a series of questions that clearly contrast our choices. Using all your understanding of what's best for kids and best for society, which option do you choose?

What do you choose?

Should schools rely on standardized content expectations and curriculum, so that all students get the same content in the same grade?	Should schools identify a clear concise set of crucial learning outcomes, and allow individual students varied amounts of time to progress along learning pathways to higher-level skills?

Or

Should teachers deliver standardized age-based content without assessing individual student learning readiness?	Should teachers use formative assessment to determine the readiness levels of each student before they begin to deliver standard content?

Or

Should instruction be time-limited, so that lessons are delivered within a set of days and all students are expected to learn the content within that timeframe, and then the teacher moves on to the next lesson?	Should instruction and support for essential content and skills continue as long as needed for each individual student to develop competency?

Or

Should "rigorous" instruction be understood to mean covering more content in the time allowed?	Should rigor be defined as knowing your students and differentiating instruction to maximize engagement and learning for each student?

Or

Should pacing guides define the rate of instruction for all students?	Should student readiness define the rate of instruction?

Or

At the end of each time-limited instructional unit, should teachers give summative assessments which sorts student by grade?	Should teachers use ongoing systematic formative assessment to understand individual student learning needs and guide instructional planning?

Or

Figure 14.1. Which Model Do You Choose?

At the end of each quarter or semester, should we summarize student learning by giving grades which sort students into winners and losers?

Or

Should teachers vigilantly monitor student learning throughout the instructional process so that instruction can be adapted to the instructional match and readiness of each child at any point in time?

Should we require students who already have certain skills and content to sit through the delivery of one-size-fits-all instruction for this same content?

Or

Should teachers be allowed to move students to more advanced learning as soon as they are ready?

When teachers notice that students are frustrated and disengaged, should they defer to the pacing guide and the one best way and continue to require students to participate in this frustrating level of instruction?

Or

When we notice students are struggling, should we adapt instruction for essential content to the student's level of readiness and allow students all the time needed to gain essential skills?

Does a grading scale based on a Bell Curve assure us that all students with a passing grade have developed deep understanding and the ability to apply the instructional content that was covered?

Or

Or are grades misleading? Are there some skills for which a B or C grade is not nearly enough? Do some skills and content deserve all the instructional time and practice needed to be learned to a level of enduring competency?

Is it ethical to sort students into learning winners and losers starting in the earliest grades during this age of learning, innovation, and technology?

Or

Is it possible to help students develop a growth mind-set by helping them understand that learning is always accessible and requires both time and effort?

Must we hold onto the familiar one-size-fits-all standardized curriculum driven system because we have invested so much time and money in the structure we have in place?

Or

Or are we ready to innovate toward a system that is designed to help all students learn at their own pace, maintain a love of learning and a growth mind-set as they continue to learn for life?

Figure 14.1.   Continued

Despite the presence of many extraordinary educators, our reliance on an antiquated design system for our schools has produced consistently inadequate results. Despite well-intentioned efforts to improve schools by creating national coverage standards and standardized assessments, too many schools have become joyless places in which there is a constant race to "cover" content and test students.

But in every corner of our nation a transformation toward competency-based learning has begun. Learning and character are the currency of the future. Our children, and students of any age, deserve a thoughtful education system that recognizes individual learning differences and offers a clear pathway to the knowledge and skills they need.

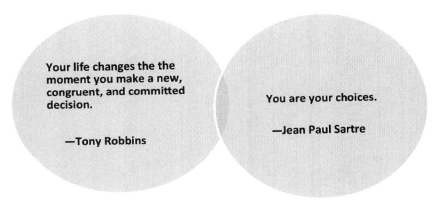

Figure 14.2.   Choices

And therefore it is time to choose. Is it time for fundamental change in the design of our learning systems?

APPENDIX

Appendix A

The Pre-K to Grade 3 Essential Math Skills Inventory

DEVELOPING A DEEP UNDERSTANDING OF BASIC MATHEMATICAL CONCEPTS

The Pre-K to Grade 3 Essential Math Skills Inventory helps you systematically measure the development of crucial basic math skills, and then respond by giving children learning activities at a level where they can be challenged and still be highly successful. It is designed for use with children aged three to nine, during the preschool to grade 3 years, because this is the period in which children have the greatest opportunity to deeply understand and fall in love with math.

Properly using this simple inventory encourages teachers and parents to know exactly which skills kids have developed to a level of deep understanding and application, and which skills still need instruction, practice, activities, projects, and/or play. By carefully tracking progress toward essential math skills, we can help almost every child deeply understand the fundamentals of math and vastly increase the number of children who use it joyfully throughout their lives.

For decades, our schools have been engaged in a failed experiment that attempts to cram more content into the time available for instruction than is humanly possible. Most schools have asked children to learn overwhelming content at younger and younger ages without carefully building the foundational skills needed for learning success.

Early childhood is the crucial time during which we build the foundation skills, behaviors, and beliefs that establish our path as a learner for life. Sadly, for many young children our teaching systems are not working effectively. By the beginning of the fourth grade, the point at which we can accurately predict long-term learning outcomes, only 40 percent of American children are at proficient math levels. By the eighth grade this has decreased to 34 percent student proficiency, and by the twelfth grade only 25 percent of students remaining in school performed at or above the proficient level in mathematics (NAEP, 2017).

The long-term effects of such numbers of American children becoming nonproficient math learners in the information age are a calamity. Low-skilled learners become low-skilled workers with low wages. Early learning success in reading and mathematics is correlated with high school graduation, going on for advanced education, better decisions about risky behaviors, decreased criminality, stable relationships, and success on the job. The costs of letting three-quarters of our children become nonproficient in math include diminished employment option for our children and reduced prosperity for our society.

It is time for us to help more of our children develop the numeracy skills that will allow them to succeed in the information economy. *The Pre-K to Grade 3 Essential Math Skills Inventory* supports teachers and parents as we stop racing through math instruction, and take the time to learn the essential outcomes well. This idea is not new.

The National Council of Teachers of Mathematics recommends that math curriculum should include fewer topics, spending enough time to make sure each is learned in enough depth that it need not be revisited in later grades. That is the approach used in most top-performing nations (National Mathematics Advisory Panel, 2008).

During the early years of math learning children should be engaged in a rich and interesting set of math learning experiences that include manipulatives, projects, and activities. Much of this early learning should seem like exploration, inquiry, and play. At school teachers are advised to use a math curriculum based on the Common Core State Standards, or on a set of outcomes developed by your state, that serve as a guide for content to cover during the year. But "covering" crucial content is not enough. Some skills need more than coverage. They need high-quality instruction, and for some children these skills require re-teaching, more time for practice, different approaches to learning, and more time for activities, which help these skills become deeply understood and easy to use in life.

Some math skills are essential to understanding numbers and how they work. These are the skills that might be considered the "core of the core." They must be well understood or a child will be forever compromised as he or she moves forward into more complex math learning.

The Pre-K to Grade 3 Essential Math Skills Inventory helps you systematically measure what matters most: student learning. It can be used along with

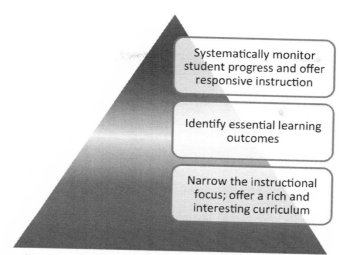

Figure Appendix A. Math Instruction Driven by Student Learning Needs

any thoughtful math curriculum or learning materials. It allows you to keep track of the skills that have been well learned, plan instruction for the skills your child is ready to learn, allow all the time needed to help him or her develop a deep understanding, and move the child forward as soon as he or she is ready for the next level of skill. During the crucial early years, we can ensure that student learning needs drive instruction rather than a nonviable curriculum or pacing guide.

With less emphasis on racing through content, we can identify essential learning outcomes and use ongoing formative assessment to keep track of how each student is progressing toward the skills that matter most. We can help children build every foundation skill to a proficient level, help more students love math, and bring more joy back into our classrooms.

THE PRE-K TO GRADE 3 ESSENTIAL
MATH SKILLS INVENTORY

Bob Sornson, PhD, Early Learning Foundation

(Pre-K) Demonstrates one-to-one correspondence for numbers 1–10, with steps

(Pre-K) Demonstrates one-to-one correspondence for numbers 1–10, with manipulatives

(Pre-K) Adds on/takes away using numbers 1–10, with steps

(Pre-K) Adds on/takes away using numbers 1–10, with manipulatives

(K) Demonstrates counting to 100

(K) Has one-to-one correspondence for numbers 1–30

(K) Understands combinations (to 10)

(K) Recognizes number groups without counting (2–10)

(1) Understands concepts of add on or take away (to 30)

(1) Adds/subtracts single digit problems on paper

(1) Counts objects with accuracy to 100

(1) Replicates visual or movement patterns

(1) Shows a group of objects by number (to 100)

(2) Quickly recognizes number groups (to 100)

(2) Adds/subtracts from a group of objects (to 100)

(2) Adds/subtracts double digit problems on paper

(2) Counts by 2, 3, 4, 5, and 10 using manipulatives

(2) Solves written and oral story problems using the correct operations

(2) Understands/identifies place value to 1,000

(3) Reads and writes numbers to 10,000 in words and numerals

(3) Uses common units of measurement:

- Length
- Weight
- Time
- Money
- Temperature

(3) Can add or subtract three digit problems on paper with regrouping

(3) Can round numbers to the 10s

(3) Can round numbers to the 100s

(3) Add and subtract 2 digit numbers mentally

(3) Counts by 5, 6, 7, 8, 9, 10 using manipulatives

(3) Uses arrays to visually depict multiplication

(3) Recognizes basic fractions

(3) Solves written and oral story problems using the correct operation

THE PRE-K TO GRADE 3 ESSENTIAL MATH SKILLS INVENTORY

Student: _____ Teacher: _____ Date: _____

Skill	Not Yet	Intervention	Developing	Proficient
Demonstrates one-to-one correspondence for numbers 1–10, with steps				
Demonstrates one-to-one correspondence for numbers 1–10, with manipulatives				
Adds on using numbers 1–10, with steps				
Adds on using numbers 1–10, with manipulatives				
Demonstrates counting to 100				
Has one-to-one correspondence for numbers 1–30				
Understands combinations (to 10)				
Recognizes number groups without counting (2–10)				
Understands concepts of add on or take away (to 30)				
Adds/subtracts single digit problems on paper				
Counts objects with accuracy to 100				
Replicates visual or movement patterns				
Shows a group of objects by number (to 100)				
Quickly recognizes number groups (to 100)				
Adds/subtracts from a group of objects (to 100)				
Adds/subtracts double digit problems on paper				
Counts by 2, 3, 4, 5, and 10 using manipulatives				
Solves written and oral story problems using the correct operations				
Understands/identifies place value to 1,000				
Reads and writes numbers to 10,000 in words and numerals				
Uses common units of measurement:				
• Length				
• Weight				
• Time				
• Money				
• Temperature				
Can add or subtract three digit problems on paper with regrouping				
Can round numbers to the 10s				
Can round numbers to the 100s				
Add and subtract 2 digit numbers mentally				
Counts by 5, 6, 7, 8, 9, 10 using manipulatives				
Uses arrays to visually depict multiplication				
Recognizes basic fractions				
Solves written and oral story problems using the correct operation				

PROTOCOL FOR USE OF THE *INDIVIDUAL ESSENTIAL MATH SKILL INVENTORY*

The *Essential Math Skills Inventory* is a simple format for systematically assessing the most crucial skills in the development of early numeracy. The inventory serves as an ongoing formative assessment tool, regularly updated by the teacher/parent, so you can identify specifically what students know and what they are ready to learn. These skills are the core of the core (CCSS) and cannot be merely "covered." These are the skills we must ensure students learn to a level of deep understanding and application. These are the foundation skills upon which a lifetime of successful mathematical learning will be built.

1. During the first few weeks of school, use observational, informal, and instructional assessment to get to know which skills your student/child has, and which skills are lagging in development.

2. Note proficiency **by writing the date** on the inventory. Student proficiency is noted only after the student has demonstrated this skill at the proficient level on several occasions and using more than one type of instructional material. Be certain that a student deeply understands and can use a skill before certifying proficiency.

3. You may wish to devise a system to remind you of the times when proficient skills were noticed. Some teachers use dots (in pencil) on the inventory to note these observations.

4. Exceptions can be made to the rule of several observations during baseline data collection, but only when teachers/parents use careful observational assessments and are certain a skill is completely proficient.

5. Plan instruction based on this information. Your knowledge regarding which skills this student already has and which ones are developing will help you pick activities and projects that match the child's readiness.

6. Update your *Essential Math Skills Inventory* weekly as you see the students move from **Intervention** to **Developing** to **Proficient**. Celebrate success.

Rubrics for measuring proficiency in the essential math skills and activities that support development of these skills can be found in *Essential Math Skills,* Shell Education, 2014, by Bob Sornson.

Appendix B

Rubric for Considering the Quality of Higher Education, Competency-Based Learning Initiatives

The issue of quality among competency-based learning systems is pressing. Some institutions of higher education, in the race to find more students or sell more credits, might choose a less demanding road to CBE. For those institutions considering a move to competency-based learning, consider this rubric for quality CBE. Level 1 describes low quality and Level 5 is highest quality.

Level 1

- A set of knowledge competencies have been established for each course
- Students work to achieve these competencies by the end of semester/year
- Students who do not achieve every competency will repeat the course

Level 2

- A set of knowledge competencies have been established for each course
- Students can test out of courses in which they have expertise and experience
- Students can move through course modules or chapters at their own pace
- Passing chapter/module tests and completion of other required assignments (papers, journals, etc.) is considered completion of course credit and/or competency
- Community service, internships, observation, performance groups, or similar experiences will be considered as the equivalent to a required course or competency

Level 3

- Competencies for each required course are clearly established, including knowledge, skill, and application

- Students are assessed to determine existing knowledge/skill/application levels, and can test out of a course by demonstrating knowledge, skill, and application
- Students have personalized learning plans focused on achieving the required learning objectives at their own pace
- Learning plans can include specific modules, learning materials, or experiences
- Students receive frequent and systematic assessment of progress
- Timely support is available
- Students advance upon demonstrated mastery of learning goals leading to required competencies

Level 4

- Minimum competencies are established for a certificate or degree, including knowledge, skill, and application
- A review/assessment of knowledge, skill, and application helps determine each student's learning needs within the program
- Personalized learning plans focus on achievement of the required competencies
- Specific short-term learning plans are developed by the facilitator and student, and can include specific modules, learning materials, or experiences
- Students receive frequent and systematic assessment of progress
- Timely support is available
- Students advance upon demonstrated mastery of learning goals leading to required competencies
- Degree or certificate is awarded upon demonstration of all required competencies

Level 5

- Minimum competencies are established for a certificate or degree, including knowledge, skill, and application
- Additional learning goals are established based on the individual needs and interests of the student
- A review/assessment of knowledge, skill, and application helps determine each student's learning needs within the program
- A review/assessment of the student's learning strengths and style helps contribute to the development of a personalized learning plan
- Personalized learning plans focus on achievement of the required competencies and the student's chosen goals
- Specific short-term learning plans are developed by the facilitator and student, and can include specific modules, learning materials, or experiences

- Cohort groups, online networks, or other support group structures are available
- Students receive frequent and systematic assessment of progress
- Timely instructional support is available
- Students advance upon demonstrated mastery of learning goals leading to required competencies and student-initiated learning goals
- Degree or certificate is awarded upon demonstration of all required competencies

Appendix C

Road Map to Personalized Competency-Based Learning

Start by doing what's necessary; then do what's possible; and suddenly you are doing the impossible.
                                                            —**St. Francis of Assisi**

Consider these ideas as you create high-quality, competency-based systems in your school or community.

Take time for preliminary planning, knowing that the process of transformation will last for years. Too often in education we adopt the newest standards without having an opportunity to even read them, or embrace a new instructional program without carefully planning for the rollout challenges. Take the time to do this work well.

Pick thoughtful contributors to this study process who represent all stakeholder groups, and allow them to do meaningful work. Examine the change from as many different perspectives as possible. Build a clear consensus around the need for transformation.

Pick a point of beginning. It might be early childhood essential outcomes, or high school graduation requirements. Decide on the competencies or outcomes that are essential, and make sure these are described precisely. Coverage standards can be vague, but competencies must be crystal clear.

Design the competency-based learning system you want. This design starts with:
- Clear competencies that articulate exactly what students need to know and be able to do
- Specific steps along the pathways to competency
- Rubrics that describe the standards for proficiency/competency/mastery at each step

- The development, purchase, and/or adaptation of an instructional plan (curriculum) and instructional materials organized around the competencies
- Assessment systems (formative and summative) that are consistent and reliable
- The role of technology for instruction
- The role of technology for assessment
- Opportunities for students to help choose learning goals above minimum expectations
- The role of the student to help design pathways to competency that match interests and learning style
- Home-school partnerships that allow parent input and to the development of learning plans and participation in the learning process
- Systems to communicate progress toward competency in the required and chosen learning goals
- Short-term and ongoing staff and community training needs

Develop a three- to five-year blueprint for implementation. If it is possible, plan on implementing change in phases. This will allow you to work out any problems that emerge in the process. Set milestones to track progress in each essential element of the plan, and create systems to track advancement toward each milestone.

Form a team to monitor and ensure progress toward your goals. Recruit stakeholders from all parts of the system/school. Teacher leaders and other employees who have the respect of the staff should be part of the transition team. Gather support for the change from all school leaders, including those who are not part of management. Make sure that the initiative is not seen as the product of a small group of visionaries, and that it is not seen as one more thing that will disappear in two to three years.

Begin training staff long before implementing the preliminary rollout. You can choose to train only those employees who will be affected first, or you can train all employees who will eventually be affected. Remember that training is more than "coverage." Helping staff develop competency in all the skills needed for CBL will include significant training over time.

Develop teacher leaders. Individual coaching and peer mentoring models can be helpful with reluctant staff members who might procrastinate, miss deadlines, or avoid the significant learning needed to become a successful competency-based instructor. By working side by side with peers who can encourage, clarify, and help them keep pace with the change process can make individuals feel more like a part of a team.

Become a learning organization. Most educators will need to develop new skills to enable them to succeed in this new model of learning. Some of these skills include, but are not limited to:
- Aligning instruction to the explicit, measurable learning objectives that make up the pathway to competency
- Providing timely, differentiated support to students based on individual learning needs, moving each student along an individual learning pathway at a sufficient pace to achieve essential learning goals
- Using formative and summative assessments to regularly assess student progress
- Developing and implementing performance-based formative and summative assessments with high validity and reliability
- Collaborating with other staff members for the development and implementation of assessment and instructional plans
- Using data on individual student learning in a timely, ongoing manner to inform instruction and support student progress to competency
- Supporting development of the whole child/student, including social and emotional competencies
- Designing and managing personalized instruction using technology, blended, or online learning, and other options
- Working with students to get input on student learning goals or a plan for pathways to competency
- Working with parents to build strong partnerships supporting the development of competency

Clear the obstacles to implementation. Identify employees or community leaders who may cause obstacles to the transition, and work with them. Identify resource issues that could interfere with your plan's implementation or success.

Put the transition plan on paper so everyone knows the blueprint for change. This plan should explain why the change is being made and what the school will look like when the transition is complete.

Proceed one step at a time. While many of us may be frustrated by the slow pace of change, the creation of personalized competency-based learning systems must be done well. Rushing through the plan sounds a lot like rushing through instruction. Take your time, help people along, ensure understanding, experiment, innovate, learn from your mistakes, and enjoy the process of creating meaningful change that will last.

Appendix D

Competency-Based Learning Resources

American Youth Policy Forum provides learning opportunities toward the development of effective youth and education policies. Their guiding principles include Student-Centered Learning, Advancement upon Mastery, Multiple Pathways to Success, and Creating Collaborative Systems that Support Youth. http://www.aypf.org/

Annie E. Casey Foundation is a private charitable organization dedicated to helping build better futures for disadvantaged children in the United States. Their work focuses on strengthening families, building stronger communities, and education issues. They have been strong advocates for the importance of preschool through grade 3 learning outcomes. http://www.aecf.org/

Carnegie Foundation for the Advancement of Teaching is a U.S.-based education policy and research center. It has conducted research on the efficacy of the practice of Carnegie Units and seat time to measure learning. http://www.carnegiefoundation.org/?s=competency+based&submit=go

Clayton Christensen Institute for Disruptive Innovation is a nonprofit, nonpartisan think tank dedicated to improving the world through disruptive innovation. The theory of disruptive innovation describes a process by which a product or service transforms an existing market by introducing simplicity, convenience, accessibility, and affordability. http://www.christenseninstitute.org/

Competency-Based Education Network (C-BEN), administered by Public Agenda, is a group of regionally accredited colleges and universities working together to address shared challenges to designing, developing, and scaling competency-based degree programs. http://www.cael.org/what-we-do/competency-based-education#sthash.gklbqi3e.dpuf

CompetencyWorks provides a variety of resources to help you understand competency education, including examples, policy, practice tips, and issue briefs. http://www.competencyworks.org/

Council for Adult & Experiential Learning is a nonprofit that works within the higher education, public, and private sectors to help adult learners get the education and training they need. With funding from Lumina Foundation for Education, the Council for Adult and Experiential Learning (CAEL) offers postsecondary institutions training on competency-based education. http://www.cael.org/what-we-do/competency-based-education

Early Learning Foundation offers training and support for school districts and parent organizations regarding PK to grade 3 personalized competency-based learning, the development of self-regulation and empathy, and parent education. Its work includes the *Essential Skill Inventories*, a competency framework for measuring ongoing progress toward essential skills in all the domains of early childhood. http://earlylearningfoundation.com/

International Association for K-12 Online Learning (iNACOL) supports the development and use of online, blended, and competency-based learning models to achieve personalized and competency-based learning, and offers a variety of reports and webinars. http://www.inacol.org/

Lumina Foundation for Education is a private, Indianapolis-based foundation. Its mission is to expand student access to and success in education beyond high school. It has sponsored a series of reports on competency-based higher education. http://www.luminafoundation.org/resources http://www.luminafoundation.org/files/resources/competency-based-education-landscape.pdf

National Assessment of Educational Progress (NAEP) is the largest continuing and nationally representative assessment of what American students know and can do in core subjects. NAEP is a congressionally mandated project administered by the National Center for Education Statistics, within the Institute of Education Sciences of the U.S. Department of Education. http://nces.ed.gov/nationsreportcard/

National Association of Elementary School Principals is a professional organization serving elementary and middle school principals and other education leaders throughout the United States, Canada, and overseas. It has developed a competency framework for effective principals working with the early childhood years. *Leading Pre-K-3 Learning Communities: Competencies for Effective Principal Practice*. https://www.naesp.org/sites/default/files/leading-pre-k-3-learning-communities-executive-summary.pdf

National Center for Competency-Based Learning (NCCBL) is a New Hampshire–based 501(c)(3) nonprofit charitable organization founded in 2013. http://www.nccbl.org/

Nellie Mae Education Foundation works with schools in New England to implement the principles of student-centered learning that is personalized, engaging, and competency-based. It offers a rich library of publications that support competency-based learning options. http://www.nmefoundation. org/resources

New Hampshire Department of Education (NHDoE) has been a leader in state competency-based learning initiatives. The NHDoE has established model literacy, mathematics, science, work/study, and arts competencies for high school graduation. http://education.nh.gov/innovations/hs_redesign/ competencies.htm

Organisation for Economic Co-operation and Development (OECD) is the sponsoring agency for the Programme for International Student Assessment (PISA). This triennial international survey evaluates education systems worldwide by testing the skills and knowledge of fifteen-year-old students. In 2012, around 510,000 students in sixty-five economies took part in the PISA 2012 assessment of reading, mathematics, and science representing about 28 million fifteen-year-olds globally. PISA is an ongoing triennial survey, allowing countries participating in successive surveys to compare their students' performance over time and assess the impact of education policy decisions. http://www.oecd.org/pisa/

Re-inventing Schools Coalition (RISC) is a division of Marzano Research. It was established by core members of the team at Chugach School District, and offers training and support materials to school districts. The history of RISC is described in *Delivering on the Promise: The Education Revolution*, by DeLorenzo, Battino, Schreiber, and Gaddy-Carrio. http://www. reinventingschools.org/

References

Chapter 1

No Child Left Behind (NCLB). (2001). Public Law PL 107-110, the No Child Left Behind Act of 2001. Retrieved at https://www2.ed.gov/nclb/landing.jhtml

Chapter 2

Christensen, Clayton M. (1997). *The innovator's dilemma: When new technologies cause great firms to fail*. Boston, MA: Harvard Business School Press.

Christensen, Clayton M., Baumann, Heiner, Ruggles, Rudy, & Sadtler, Thomas M. (2006). "Disruptive innovation for social change." *Harvard Business Review*, December 2006.

Christensen, Clayton M., Scott, Anthony D., & Roth, Erik A. (2004). *Seeing what's next*. Cambridge, MA: Harvard Business School Press.

Chapter 3

National Assessment of Educational Progress. (2013). Retrieved at http://nationsreportcard.gov/reading_math_g12_2013/#/

The Nation's Report Card: Trends in Academic Progress. (2012). Retrieved at https://nces.ed.gov/nationsreportcard/pubs/main2012/2013456.aspx

Institute of Education Sciences/ The National Center for Education Research (NCER), Implementation and Impact Evaluation of Race to the Top and School Improvement Grants. (2017). Retrieved at: https://ies.ed.gov/ncee/projects/evaluation/other_racetotop.asp.

Chapter 4

Sornson, B. (2012a). *Essential skill inventories PK-3*. Brighton, MI: Early Learning Foundation.

Sornson, B. (2012a). *Essential skill inventories PK-3*. Brighton, MI: Early Learning Foundation.

Chapter 5

Annie E. Casey Foundation. (2010). *Early warning! Why reading by the end of third grade matters*. Baltimore, MD: Annie E. Casey Foundation.

DeLorenzo, R., Battino, W., Schreiber, R., & Gaddy-Carrio, B. (2008). *Delivering on the promise*. Bloomington, IN: Solution Tree.

Fielding, L., Kerr, N., & Rosier, P. (2007). *Annual growth for all students, catch up growth for those who are behind*. Kennewick, WA: The New Foundation Press.

Hernandez, Donald. (2011). *Double jeopardy: How third-grade reading skills and poverty influence high school graduation*. Baltimore, MD: Annie E. Casey Foundation.

Mississippi Department of Education. (2016). Preschool Assessment Result for Early Learning Collaboratives. Retrieved at http://www.mde.k12.ms.us/docs/student-assessment/kreadiness-and-prek-2016-17.pdf?sfvrsn=2

National Center for Education Statistics. (2016). *The Nation's Report Card, 2015 Reading Trial Urban District Snapshot Report Detroit, Grade 4, Public Schools*. NCES. Retrieved at https://nces.ed.gov/nationsreportcard/subject/publications/dst2015/pdf/2016048xr4.pdf

New York State Department of Education. (2016). Spring 2016 Grades 3–8 ELA and Math Assessment Results. Retrieved at http://www.nysed.gov/news/2016/state-education-department-releases-spring-2016-grades-3-8-ela-and-math-assessment-results

Snow, C.E., Burns, S., & Griffin, P., eds. (1998). *Preventing reading difficulties in young children, Report of the Committee on the Prevention of Reading Difficulties in Young Children*. Washington, DC: National Academy Press.

Sornson, B. (2012a). *Essential skills inventories PK-3*. Brighton, MI: Early Learning Foundation.

Sornson, B. (2012b). *Fanatically formative: Successful learning during the crucial K-3 years*. Thousand Oaks, CA: Corwin Press.

Sornson, B. (2014). *Essential math skills*. Huntington Beach, CA: Shell Education.

Sornson, B. (2015). "The effects of using the Essential Skills Inventory on teacher perception of high-quality classroom instruction." *Preventing School Failure: Alternative Education for Children and Youth*, 59: 3, 161–167.

Sornson, Bob, & Davis, Debbie. (2013). "Focus on essential learning outcomes." *Journal of Research Initiatives*, 1: 1, Article 8, http://digitalcommons.uncfsu.edu/jri/vol1/iss1/8.

Torgesen, J. K. (1998). "Catch them before they fail." *American Educator*, 22: 1–2, 32–39.

Torgesen, J. K. (2002). "The prevention of reading difficulties." *Journal of School Psychology*, 40, 7–26.

Chapter 6

ACT (2013). *The Reality of College Readiness*. National Version. Retrieved at https://files.eric.ed.gov/fulltext/ED546858.pdf

ACT Profile Report – National (2017). Retrieved at https://www.act.org/content/dam/act/unsecured/documents/cccr2017/P_99_999999_N_S_N00_ACT-GCPR_National.pdf

Branmante, F. & Colby, R. (2012). *Off the clock: Moving education from time to competency.* Thousand Oaks, CA: Sage Publications.

Educational Testing Service (2015). *America's Skills Challenge: Millennials and the Future.* Retrieved at http://www.ets.org/s/research/30079/asc-millennials-and-the-future.pdf

European Commission. (2007). *Key Competences for Lifelong Learning.* European Reference Framework Luxembourg: Office for Official Publications of the European Communities. Retrieved at http://eur-lex.europa.eu/LexUriServ/LexUriServ.do?uri=OJ:L:2006:394:0010:0018:EN:PDF

Maine Department of Education. (2012). *Education Evolving: Maine's Plan for Putting Learners First.* Retrieved at http://maine.gov/doe/plan

Mission: Readiness (2009). *Ready, Willing, And Unable To Serve.* Retrieved at http://cdn.missionreadiness.org/NATEE1109.pdf or at https://strongnation.s3.amazonaws.com/documents/3/ad129721-81c2-430e-a0a9-7261 1ec2ad1c.pdf?1469801577&inline;%20filename=%22Ready%20Willing%20and%20Unable_NATIONAL.pdf%22

National Assessment of Educational Progress. (2013). *The Nation's Report Card 2013.* Retrieved at http://nationsreportcard.gov/reading_math_g12_2013/#/

National Assessment of Educational Progress. (2015). *The Nation's Report Card 2015.* Retrieved at https://www.nationsreportcard.gov/reading_math_2015/#?grade=4

World Economic Forum. (2016). *The Future of Jobs.* Retrieved at https://www.weforum.org/reports/the-future-of-jobs

Chapter 8

Hattie, J. (2009). *Visible learning.* New York: Routledge Press.

Kanigel, Robert. (1997). *The one best way: Frederick Winslow Taylor and the enigma of efficiency.* New York: Viking.

National Mathematics Advisory Council. (2008). Foundations for Success: The Final Report of the National Mathematics Advisory Council. Washington, DC: U.S. Department of Education.

Schmidt, W. H., & Cogan, L. S. (2009). "The myth of equal content." *Educational Leadership,* 67: 3, 44–47.

Schmidt, W. H., McKnight, C. C., Houang, R. T., Wang, H. C., Wiley, D. E., Cogan, L. S., & Wolfe, R. G. (2001). *Why schools matter: A cross-national comparison of curriculum and learning.* San Francisco, CA: Jossey-Bass.

Schmidt, W. H., Wang, H. A., & McKnight, C. C. (2005). "Curriculum coherence: An examination of U.S. mathematics and science content standards from an international perspective." *Journal of Curriculum Studies,* 37: 5, 525–529.

Schmoker, M., & Marzano, R. J. (1999, March). Realizing the promise of standards-based education. *Educational Leadership,* 56(6), 17–21.

Senge, Peter M. (1994). *The fifth discipline: The art and practice of the learning organization.* New York: Doubleday.

Chapter 9

Barber, M., & Mourshed, M. (2007). *How the world's best-performing school systems come out on top.* London: McKinsey and Company.

Cushman School. (2017). *Our Mission and Philosophy*. Retrieved from https://www. cushmanschool.org/about-cushman/our-mission-philosophy/

Chapter 10

Sornson, B. (2007). "The early learning success initiative." *Educational Leadership*, 65: 2, 42–43.

Sornson, B., Frost, F. & Burns, M. (2005). "Instructional support teams in Michigan." *Communique'*, 33: 5, 28–29 .

Chapter 11

Csíkszentmihályi, Mihály. (1996). *Finding flow: The psychology of engagement with everyday life*. New York: Basic Books.

Fredrickson, B. L. (1998). "What good are positive emotions?" *Review of General Psychology*, 2, 300–319.

Fredrickson, B. L. (2001). "The role of positive emotions in positive psychology: The broaden-and-build theory of positive emotions." *American Psychologist*, 56, 218–226.

Fredrickson, B. L. (2003). "The value of positive emotions." *American Scientist*, 91, 330–335.

Fredrickson, B. L. (2009). *Positivity*. New York, NY: Crown.

Fredrickson, B. L. & Losada, M. F. (2005). "Positive affect and the complex dynamics of human flourishing." *American Psychologist*, 60: 7, 678–686.

Hawking, S. (1998). *A brief history of time*. New York: Bantam Books.

Maslow, A. H. (1954). *Motivation and personality*. New York: Harper and Row.

Robinson, Ken. (2013). How to Escape Education's Death Valley, TED. Retrieved at https://www.ted.com/talks/ken_robinson_how_to_escape_education_s_death_valley?language=en

Wolk, Steven. (2008). "Joy in school." *Educational Leadership*, 66: 1, 8–15.

Chapter 12

Derringer, Nancy. (2017). "Fewer college students want to be teachers, and why it matters." *Bridge Magazine*, August 3, 2017. Retrieved at http://www.bridgemi.com/talent-education/fewer-college-students-want-be-teachers-and-why-it-matters-searchable-database

Eagan, K., Stolzenberg, E. B., Zimmerman, H. B., Aragon, M. C., Whang Sayson, H., & RiosAguilar, C. (2016). *The American Freshman: National Norms Fall 2016*, UCLA School of Education. Retrieved at www.heri.ucla.edu

Ingersoll, R. M. (2001). "Teacher turnover and teacher shortages: An organizational analysis." *American Educational Research Journal*, 37: 3, 499–534.

Ingersoll, R. M. (2002). "The teacher shortage: A case of wrong diagnosis and wrong prescription." *NASSP Bulletin*, 86: 631, 16–30. Retrieved at www.principals.org/news/bltn_teachshort0602.html

Sutcher, Leib, Darling-Hammond, Linda, & Carver-Thomas, Desiree. (2016). *A Coming Crisis in Teaching? Teacher Supply, Demand, and Shortages in the U.S.*, Learning Policy Institute. Retrieved at https://learningpolicyinstitute.org/product/coming-crisis-teaching

About the Author

 **Bob Sornson** is a best-selling author and international consultant whose work focuses on early learning success, high-quality competency-based learning, and parenting.

Born and raised in Detroit along with his six siblings, Bob earned a bachelor's and master's degree at the University of Michigan, an education specialist degree from Central Michigan University, and his PhD from Andrews University. For over thirty years he worked as a teacher and as an administrator in Michigan public schools, developed an acclaimed model early learning success initiative, and in 2001 founded the *Early Learning Foundation*.

A prolific author, Bob has written best-selling books for educators, parents, and children, along with many journal publications. His books include *Over-Tested and Under-Prepared* (Routledge), *Essential Math Skills* (Shell Education), *Fanatically Formative* (Corwin Press), *Stand in My Shoes: Kids Learning about Empathy* (Love and Logic Press), *The Juice Box Bully* (Early Learning Foundation Press), *Teaching and Joy* (ASCD), and *Creating Classrooms Where Teachers Love to Teach and Students Love to Learn* (Love and Logic Press). He has offered workshops and keynotes in forty-eight states.

He lives with his wife Nancy in Brighton, Michigan, and can be contacted at earlylearningfoundation.com.

Made in the USA
Middletown, DE
31 October 2018